"Kim Cameron-Smith presents a wonderful model for parenting that allows moms and dads to be true mentors to their children. She offers practical, faithful suggestions that will help parents capture their children's hearts and bring them to God."

— Dr. Greg Popcak, author, radio host, counselor, and founder and executive director of the Pastoral Solutions Institute

"Kim Cameron-Smith's *Discipleship Parenting: Planting the Seeds of Faith* provides simple, straightforward, realistic advice that helps us go from surviving to thriving, all while keeping our eyes focused on Christ. If we want to find the building blocks for raising a truly beautiful domestic church in today's tumultuous world, this is the book that's going to get us going."

— Tommy Tighe, co-host of *Repent and Submit* on CatholicTV

D1605773

Discipleship Parenting

Discipleship
Parenting

Planting the
Seeds of Faith

Kim Cameron-Smith

Our Sunday Visitor
Huntington, Indiana

Our Sunday Visitor Publishing Division
Our Sunday Visitor, Inc.
200 Noll Plaza
Huntington, IN 46750
www.osv.com
1-800-348-2440

ISBN: 978-1-68192-352-9 (Inventory No. T2036)
1. FAMILY & RELATIONSHIPS—Parenting—General. 2. RELIGION—Christian Living—Family & Relationships. 3. RELIGION—Christianity—Catholic.

eISBN: 978-1-68192-353-6
LCCN: 2019948061

Cover and interior design: Lindsey Riesen
Cover art: Shutterstock

PRINTED IN THE UNITED STATES OF AMERICA

For my husband, Philip,
who always thinks my ideas sound
interesting and sensible,
including when I wanted a pet goat.

And for our children,
Aidan, Claire, Dominic, and Lydia,
who taught me to understand what is
beautiful and real,
and how to take down any opponent in arm wrestling.

Contents

Introduction
11

Love
27

Balance
61

Play
85

Merciful Discipline
103

Empathy
143

Radiant Faith
169

A Strong Marriage
205

Conclusion
233

Notes
239

Introduction

The history of mankind, the history of salvation, passes by way of the family. ... The family is placed at the center of the great struggle between good and evil, between life and death, between love and all that is opposed to love.

SAINT JOHN PAUL THE GREAT

When we become parents, we have little to no experience. We are presented after nine months of pregnancy, and a select number of hours of labor and delivery, with a sweet, indescribably beautiful baby. There she (or he!) is: BORN. Blinking and hungry, this tiny human needs us so completely that it's both exhilarating and a little frightening. None of us can forget meeting our baby for the first time after many months of wondering what she would look like and how she would feel in our arms. Even though all four of my children were born by C-section (my first was an emergency surgery), I vividly remember my first glimpse of each of their faces and hearing their first calls. With each one of them, I spent the first hours after delivery simply staring at them, drinking in their newness, mesmerized by their hands, ears, and feet — madly in love already.

What we experience in those minutes and hours just after birth often deepens our understanding of and appreciation

11

for the transcendent. We know something astonishing has just happened, even if we're not sure exactly what it is. We seem to hover outside time, and, for a moment, it's like we brush up against the door to heaven. Adoptive parents experience something similar when, after months of dreaming and waiting, they finally embrace their child. In a moment, they are transformed.

No doubt parenting gives us an appreciation for the gift of life and even a deep sense of purpose. But at some point in our parenting journey, many of us become a little lost or even discouraged. We all have hopes and dreams for our children on that first day we meet them, but we commonly lose sight of those hopes and dreams for any number of reasons. Perhaps we're parenting our kids the way we were parented, or the way our friends are parenting; yet we know something isn't working. Or maybe our child came to us with special sensitivities and needs, and we're still figuring out how to live together peacefully. Or maybe life seems to have swept our family away in a wave of constant activity, appointments, and classes. It's exhausting, and we wonder whether this is really good for our children. Whatever the reason, we seem merely to muddle along, taking things as they come, responding to crises as they erupt. Unfortunately, this is parenting in triage mode and it's not ideal, because it's parenting in retrospect, parenting by repair. Especially given the culture in which we're raising our children — a culture that devalues and even ridicules strong, traditional families and looks upon children as disposable inconveniences — our private hopes for our children will only be realized with serious commitment and divine assistance.

The Great Commission of Parenting

It's important that we Catholic parents remain intentional in our parenting, that we keep in mind "the big picture." We should ask ourselves deeper questions than the larger society is asking. Let's face it: The larger society asks shallow ques-

tions that will get us nowhere. "Who's the next 'Bachelor'?"
"Have you seen my leather seats?" "Are my eyelashes long
enough?" These questions are not important. When God entrusted our children to us, he gave us an immeasurable gift,
so let's ask ourselves what he wants from us in return. What is
our mission as Catholic parents? What does our mission call
us to do? What is our specific, deepest purpose as parents of
these particular children?

- Our mission is to raise children who know and
  love God.
- Our mission is to raise children with searching
  hearts who continue growing spiritually for the
  rest of their lives.
- Our mission is to raise children who possess a
  heroic fidelity to the Truth, so they cannot help
  but share that message with others in charity.

This is called discipleship. In collaboration with Christ
through grace, our deepest purpose is to become disciple-parents, to evangelize our children so that they become disciples
themselves. This is our real purpose in this parenting journey.

Of course, every Christian is called to discipleship. Sacred
Scripture records Christ's last words to his disciples before the
Ascension: "Go therefore and make disciples of all nations,
baptizing them in the name of the Father and of the Son and
of the Holy Spirit, teaching them to observe all that I have
commanded you" (Mt 28:19–20a). This is known as the "Great
Commission." With these words, Christ instructs his disciples to make other disciples just as he made them: by living in
community with them, eating with them, laughing with them,
correcting them, and teaching them. Christ instructs his disciples to go about their lives and show people his truth and
light through their example. Today, like those first disciples,
we are called to proclaim the Good News. Through ordinary

relationships, we are to be witnesses to the renewal and peace available to all who choose to follow Christ.

If all Christians are called to make disciples, then the "Great Commission of Parenting" is to evangelize our own children.[1] This is primarily our responsibility — not the responsibility of the director of religious education (DRE) at our parish. The DRE and the faith-formation program are there to support us in evangelizing our kids, not to replace us. With all the tasks that keep us busy as parents, it's easy to forget that faith formation is our most important duty to our children. It's more important than any other goal we may have for our kids. It's more important than their grades, which position they play on the high school football team, or where they go to college. Yes, I hope my kids do well in school, and I hope they will be successful. These are not unreasonable hopes. But my deepest hope for my children is that they spend eternity with God, and that they come to know and abide in the Truth, even in a world that increasingly denies truth exists.

Our mission isn't limited to teaching our children the facts of the Faith (though this is an essential part of it). Ideally, we participate with God in fanning the flames of love within our children's hearts for him and his Church. We want our children to possess wisdom and zeal. I hope my kids aren't just committed to the Church; I hope their relationship with God grows deeper for the rest of their lives.

During his earthly ministry, Christ always had some followers who tended to stand at the back of the room, watching him from a distance. They were intrigued by Jesus, yes, but not really willing to be changed by him. They observed but did not engage. These followers quickly fell away when their own comfort was threatened. Then there were other followers who were compelled to draw close to Christ. They recognized that what he was saying shattered much of what they once knew, but still they leaned forward and listened. They found answers to their most burning questions in his message and way of life.

What he said made them uncomfortable, but they couldn't turn away.

One of my favorite moments in Sacred Scripture comes during the Discourse on the Bread of Life in the Gospel of John. Jesus has just shared the hard teaching that his followers will have to eat his flesh and drink his blood. This is so shocking to Jewish ears that some of Jesus' followers abandon him. Jesus turns to his inner circle of friends and asks if they want to go away, too. Peter answers, "Lord, to whom shall we go? You have the words of eternal life" (Jn 6:66–68). Peter has surrendered to Jesus. *What can I do, Lord? You're IT for me.* Though they were imperfect, Jesus' friends continued to love him even when what he said was shocking, and probably embarrassing. Save Judas, they couldn't abandon him, because they had experienced a conversion of mind, heart, and spirit.

None of us wants our kids to be part of that back-room crowd that freaks out when the going gets tough or when their personal comfort zones are challenged. When the very foundation of society has been threatened by moral relativism, we want our kids to have moral chops and a growing affection for and devotion to Christ and his Church. Of course, we can't make this happen by magic, or as an executive order to our kids. ("Okay, guys, next up on the to-do list: it's time to get very excited about God. I'd like to see that done by 8:30, thanks.") Just like any discipleship relationship, we evangelize our children by living side by side with them, eating with them, laughing with them, correcting them, and teaching them. We evangelize our children through the laundry folding, diaper changing, nose wiping, and tantrum taming. We don't have to conquer these things before we can get on with the task of evangelizing our children, because these ordinary family experiences are essential to what we might call the "little way of family discipleship."

The family is the first and most perfect place to shape a child's love for Christ. As I will show in this book, a child's first relationships in his family are foundational for his openness to the love of God, and for his continued spiritual growth throughout life. What's even more extraordinary is that it's through living together as a family that Christ continues to form us all as his disciples — not just the children, but parents, too. I'm astonished at how God loves me and reveals his will for me through my own parenting. God teaches us through our teaching, loves us through our loving, evangelizes us through our evangelizing, and parents us through our parenting. My own family, and each of our families, can walk on a path of discipleship together, living in communion, serving as a light to other families.

Modern Obstacles to Raising Faithful Kids

One of my graduate school professors, a Catholic priest, often reflected on his upbringing in New York City in his working-class Irish Catholic family. Dad was a cop; Mom raised five children and worked occasionally as a typist. His family's social life revolved around their parish. I imagine that when he was a boy, my professor knew every inch of his parish, encountered the joys and sorrows in the lives of the people in his parish, and personally identified with the space, smells, sounds, and traditions of his Catholic upbringing.

Catholic culture and the tenets of our Faith permeated my professor's early life. His experience was not unusual for people of his generation in the mid-twentieth century, especially among immigrant families who tended to live in close-knit communities. Catholicism was the glue that held many neighborhoods together, providing schools, medical care, sports leagues, unions, and even newspapers. We cannot underestimate the power and effectiveness of that former structure in transmitting the Faith to children. It was a natural, uncomplicated way to give the next generation a firm Catholic identity.

Things have changed. We tend to live isolated lives; we are isolated not just from our parishes but even from our neighbors. Individualism and materialism are a persistent blight on the spiritual vibrancy of the Church, making it difficult to nourish the faith life of the laity, including children. Society has become increasingly secularized and even hostile to the idea of a divine creator. Secularists aggressively shove God to the outermost margins of society and culture, seeing God as a threat to human freedom and flourishing, rather than the answer to it.

It's easy to overlook these trends or assume they aren't relevant to us and our families. But the statistics are sobering. Young adults today are twice as likely to describe themselves as agnostic, atheist, or religiously unaffiliated than young adults thirty or forty years ago.[2] They just don't see religion as being relevant to their lives. Those young people who do believe in God often have a smorgasbord mentality about faith; they shop around for the most entertaining place to get their "faith fix." When their perceived needs are not met, they move on, never developing a sense of belonging to any faith community and never finding an answer to their emptiness.

Because of these social changes, Catholic children no longer possess the visceral rootedness in the Catholic faith experienced by previous generations. Archbishop Charles Chaput urges us "to encourage the seeds of renewal that can enliven our young people."[3] Unfortunately, we are struggling to nourish the seeds of faith in our kids, because the soil in which we're planting has become hardened and hostile to new life. Certainly we all have great hopes for our children, yet when it comes to raising faithful kids against these incredible odds, hope needs legs. If we want to fulfill our mission of raising faith-filled followers of Jesus, we have to find a way to sow the seeds of faith in fertile soil, not in rocks, weeds, and hard clay. How do we accomplish this?

Our Little Seminaries

In his marvelous book *When the Church Was Young*, Marcellino D'Ambrosio offers an intriguing account of the friendship between the three great Cappadocian Fathers of the Church: Basil the Great, Gregory of Nyssa (Basil's younger brother), and Gregory of Nazianzus (Basil's friend from childhood). These three men had a profound impact on Christianity through their development of systematic theology and clarification of several central Catholic doctrines. One might wonder which seminary these fine scholars attended, but D'Ambrosio points out that no seminaries existed at the time. Yet they were all holy, intellectually gifted priests. Where did the seeds of these gifts grow? At home. The family environment in their childhood homes created the perfect seminary.

I believe D'Ambrosio's insight is so important for this discussion that I'll quote him at length:

> The word *seminary* means greenhouse, the place of ideal growing conditions where seeds can sprout and seedlings can be nurtured before being transplanted into the harsher conditions of the outdoors. Clearly, it was two Cappadocian families and the friendships that united them which provided the fertile soil for the germination of sanctity, genius, and priestly vocation in each of these three great men. Behind these Fathers of the Church stand holy parents, grandparents, brothers, and sisters who clearly played a decisive role in all they accomplished. The pastoral implications of the Cappadocian experience are considerable: the family as domestic church, parents as primary educators of their children, the urgent need to recover and deepen the ideal of the Christian family even as society seeks to dismantle it.[4]

I feel a swell of possibility when I read this. Our homes as the domestic church really do serve as the first seminary for our children. If we understand our homes this way, our path forward as Christian parents becomes a little clearer. It's true, we can't do things the "old way"; the soil is depleted of nutrients; seeds sowed in it will probably ultimately wither. But there is another way, a better way. Like the Cappadocian families, we, too, can nourish our home environments so that the seeds of our children's faith are planted in rich soil where they can germinate and flourish. Despite the challenges, we can raise children who are holy, faithful, passionate Christians. Our children each have a special vocation and mission, and within our little seminaries, they can find their way to joy and sanctity through the foundations we provide them.

Fertile Soil: The Seven Building Blocks

What are the ideal growing conditions to nourish the seeds of faith in our homes, so that those seeds can germinate and become strong enough to survive the harsher conditions beyond our doors? How do we create little seminaries in the twenty-first century? This book provides my answers to that question. I believe we can evangelize our children by (1) building and protecting trust and connection between ourselves and our kids; (2) attending to the emotional well-being of our kids; and (3) creating a vibrant, beautiful Catholic home culture. The "Seven Building Blocks to a Joyful Catholic Home," which I explain in later chapters, provide a clear structure for moving toward this ideal.

I think we all understand why it is beneficial to create a strong Catholic culture in our homes, given the aggressive secularization of the broader culture and society. I will focus on how we create such a culture in chapter 6. But why do I mention trust, connection, and emotional well-being? What do these have to do with evangelizing our children? This proposition probably requires more explanation.

Hold On to Your Kids

It's important for us to remember that the first disciples — Jesus' inner circle of twelve — *wanted* to be taught. They wanted to follow him; he didn't kidnap them! The disciples watched Jesus: they observed how he prayed, how he paced his life, how he interacted with people from many different walks of life, and how he responded to challenges from authorities. They asked him to teach them to pray because they saw him doing it, so they wanted to do it, too. They watched him ... and they wanted to be like him. That's what we need in the environment of our little seminaries. We need to foster a similar trust and connection between ourselves and our children.

If we have any hope of evangelizing them, our children have to *want* to follow us. They must be comfortable turning to us for help and clarity like Jesus' friends turned to him. However, kids today, particularly teenagers, frequently tune out their parents and turn to their friends to provide answers to their deepest questions. Worse, parents frequently assume their teens' obsession with being in constant contact with friends through social media and instant messaging must be normal and healthy. It is not.

Although it is natural for older kids and teens to be interested in friendships and deepening their social bonds, we parents must still be their primary role models as they seek to define their values. In fact, this is how it was throughout history until recent decades.[5] We are parenting in a time unique in history: Our children look to each other for signals about what is valuable and what deserves their attention and respect. Disastrous. If a child's bond with a friend is stronger than with his parents, that child will likely choose the friend over the parents. Such a child would rather lose the respect of his parents than threaten the always fragile connection to a peer. The parents' opinions, values, and authority will mean little to such a child.

In short, despite popular opinion to the contrary, it is not healthy for kids to look to one another for cues about what is good, beautiful, and true. If we want to raise disciples, we have to hold on to our kids, not let them go. We have to remain the go-to people for our kids as they navigate childhood and the teen years. If they don't follow us, we can't lead them. If we can't lead them, we will never evangelize them.

The Whole Child and His Heart for Christ

Some secular parenting books provide terrific insights into the way family environment shapes the way children develop emotionally, but many of them lack the spiritual wisdom that Christian parents long for and need. We need to know how optimal development and healthy home relationships relate to our child's (and our own) faith life. Many Christian parenting books, on the other hand, provide a recipe for raising God-fearing, faith-filled children, but they too often overlook a central truth: Children will mature spiritually only to the extent that they are emotionally whole.

To nurture our children's faith today, we must understand not only such things as which saints' books or children's catechism we should read to them (both very important questions!), but also how the process of healthy child development intersects with the stages of spiritual growth. As I will explain in the next chapter, a child's early relationship with his parents creates an internal working model for all his relationships, including his relationship with God. That internal working model makes it either easier or harder for him to leave the crowd at the back of the room in order to move ever closer to Christ where he can become his true follower.

This is why I believe we must attend not only to our Catholic home culture, but also to our children's emotional flourishing and to the quality of the connection we have with them. A beautiful Catholic home culture is necessary, but not on its own sufficient, for raising disciples. In today's world, we need to ensure the culture we create matters to and nourishes them. And we do that by attending to their emotional wellness and to their connection with us.

This is my vision of discipleship parenting, and I believe we can accomplish it if we attend to these seven areas in our homes:

1. Love
2. Balance
3. Play
4. Merciful Discipline
5. Empathy
6. Radiant Faith
7. A Strong Marriage

Over the years I have refined these Seven Building Blocks, particularly as my kids have matured, but I believe they are an important contribution toward understanding how to create that greenhouse environment in which to grow a deep and resilient faith in our children. Of course, there are no guarantees. Our children could grow up in a beautiful Catholic home, surrounded by warm, encouraging parents and siblings, yet still make the wrong choices in life. We are raising children, not programming robots. However, I do believe we can make it easier for our children to cross the bridge to discipleship if we cooperate with God in shaping their hearts when they are young.

Catholic Social Doctrine for Families

The Seven Building Blocks are inspired by and are a practical application of two principles of Catholic social doctrine: the *principle of solidarity* and the *principle of the common good*. The *principle of solidarity* emphasizes both the dignity of the human person and our intrinsic need for interdependence rather than radical independence.[6] I affirm throughout this book the shared human dignity of all family members and our inborn need, especially at home, for intimate companionship, compassion, and support. The Seven Building Blocks are neither child-centered nor parent-centered: They are family-centered. Although the needs of the smallest and weakest members of the family are naturally prioritized, I take into account the increasing capacity of children, as they mature, to contribute to the smooth running of the household.[7] In order to grow spiritually, our children actually *need* the opportunity to serve our families. In our little seminaries, the gifts of all are valued and shared.

The *principle of the common good* indicates "'the sum total of social conditions which allow people, either as groups or as individuals, to reach their fulfillment more fully and more easily.' The common good concerns the life of all. It calls for prudence from each, and even more from those who exercise the office of authority" (*Catechism of the Catholic Church* [CCC] 1906). Disciple-parents work toward the common good by asking themselves what conditions are necessary for the fulfillment of their family as a whole and each individual member within it. The Seven Building Blocks partly took shape through my own journey toward understanding those conditions.

I write not as a perfect parent who has all the answers, but as a wounded parent who has searched for answers. Through providence, I have found some answers in surprising places and in the words of many people wiser than I. I hope they provide some insight for you, too.

As we proceed, here's a sketch of each building block, and an overview of where we're heading, in each of the following chapters.

Love

A house is only as good as its foundation. In order to continue maturing spiritually, our children need to possess hearts that are drawn to the truth, and they need to be capable of authentic love. In this chapter, I explain why our homes must be built on a foundation of warmth and deep connection, and how we can work toward that ideal even as imperfect parents.

Balance

Exterior walls create the basic footprint of a house, providing both the limits and the possibilities for how the interior space can be used. Balance is a lot like that. How we choose to fill our family calendar can create outlets for exploration, fun, and growth, but it can also lead to burnout and disconnection. In this chapter, I provide tips for discerning how to use your time wisely for the benefit of your whole family and especially for the kingdom of God. Through our modeling and mentoring, we can teach our children that time is a gift from God, and that we use our time as a family to glorify him.

Play

Play is like a window that invites daylight and fresh air into our homes. The desire and drive to play is built into the design God gave our bodies. We all need play, especially children. In this chapter, I explain how play helps kids work through their fears and frustrations, gain self-confidence, and even understand God a little better. Family play is one of the best ways to build rapport and trust between a parent and child, and between the child and God.

Merciful Discipline

Merciful discipline is like the interior walls in a home. It provides structure and boundaries, as well as doors for welcoming one another and building bonds. Effective discipline begins before behavioral problems emerge: It begins with understanding the child's immaturity and the common triggers for misbehavior. In this chapter, I provide an overview of the developmental goals of each stage of childhood. With this understanding, we can keep many behavioral issues from emerging in the first place. When behavioral issues do come up, I offer some effective tools for addressing the behavior while also guiding the child toward greater emotional and spiritual integration.

Empathy

In a house, interior lighting allows us to see one another better, especially when it's dark. Empathy is like that: It is the gift we use to know other persons — to understand their experiences, to recognize their perspectives, even when they differ from our own. In this chapter, I explain why empathy is critical to spiritual maturation, why it's endangered in our culture, and how we can raise children who possess it.

Radiant Faith

Radiant faith is like the front door to a home. Through it, our children can find their best passage to the larger world. Here I touch on how to nourish a child's faith life at different developmental stages. I discuss the importance of creating a warm Catholic home culture that will become part of a child's identity and sense of history. I'll offer some ideas for celebrating the liturgical seasons at home, creating a family altar, and finding a family prayer routine.

A Strong Marriage

No matter how expensive the upgrades inside, a house is only as secure as its roof. Granite countertops can't keep out rain and wind! Marriage is the roof on a family: Our family will be only as stable and healthy as our marriage. Kids need us to nourish our marriage, because it models for them how to treat others in intimate relationships. In this chapter, I'll share what I've learned about the sacramental power of marriage and how grace can carry us through rough patches.

In reading this book, may you come to see yourself as a disciple-parent clearing the spiritual ground of your home of the weeds and strangling vines that prevent new life from growing. With the ground prepared, your family will spend less time bogged down in distractions, division, or chaos, while you become increasingly free to recognize, understand, and respond to God's call and mission for your family on your path of discipleship.

Okay, let's dive in!

CHAPTER ONE

Love

We begin at the real beginning, with love as the Divine energy.
C. S. LEWIS, *THE FOUR LOVES*

Many parishes are beginning to recover an understanding of the vital role of the laity in evangelization, and some parish ministries have a renewed sense of purpose as they shift their focus to evangelizing disengaged Catholics and nonbelievers. These leaders are asking themselves how many real disciples are registered in their parishes. Responding to the increasing need for support in these parishes, some dioceses are rolling out formal programs for turning the laity into effective disciple-makers. This intentional focus on leading others to truth and to a real relationship with Christ is very exciting!

Of course, we should be careful not to become distracted from the true nature of discipleship. Sometimes I sense that we're searching zealously for the perfect program, as if the program will make the disciples. Programs are appealing because they allow us to feel in control, like we're doing something productive. And they do provide a helpful framework when we have no idea what we're doing. But hopefully we don't forget that true discipleship will always point others toward a Person, not a program.

Christ asks us to take a risk. He wants us to love people into discipleship. The love required for disciple-making requires more than a great PowerPoint presentation or beautifully designed program materials (though these are very good tools). Christ calls us to make disciples within the context of real-life human relationships, with all the drama, mess, and unpredictability that come with them.

I guess it's a good idea to pay attention to the number of disciples in our parishes. After all, Jesus counted his disciples. We should remember, though, that discipleship is ultimately about the quality, not the quantity, of our relationships. This is the way Christ wants it. Why? Because discipleship will happen only when others trust us, and others will trust us only when they truly know us and feel known by us. This takes time. This takes vulnerability.

Discipleship Love

To be a disciple, we must be capable of self-giving love — what philosophers call *agape*. Agape puts the good of the other first, even before our own interests … even if we don't particularly like the other person. This is very difficult, to say the least. It runs counter to our fallen nature. Jesus became man partly to show us how to love like this. He is Agape Perfected.

I think most parents have experienced agape. We're willing to suffer in ways we never imagined before becoming parents. We sacrifice sleep, our careers, our waistlines, and even regular showers, all for the good of our kids. And what a privilege it is to love like this. Our children, lush-lashed and chubby-cheeked, help us practice agape so that we can offer it to other (often less appealing) people. When we offer a beautiful act of generosity to someone in need, because they need it, even if they don't particularly deserve it, we are practicing agape.

However, discipleship requires even more from us than self-giving love. It requires a capacity for what I'll call "we-giving love." This is "mutuality" or *philia*.[1] Communal in nature, mutuality is a sharing in the life of others in friendship or community; it's a commitment to their well-being and a willingness to be changed by them. Each person both gives and receives love freely in the relationship (rather than one person doing all the giving while others do all the receiving). This is the model of love between Christ and his inner circle of disciples.

The path of discipleship is very crowded with people for a reason. We work out our identity and unique mission as a disciple through agape and philia within a community of people. Imperfect, sometimes wonderful, oftentimes exasperating people. It's hard to love like this. The love of discipleship requires freedom — a kind of freedom that exists only in a heart that is open and ready for genuine encounter in relationships. Not everyone becomes a disciple, in part because not everyone possesses this freedom. Some of us don't really want to know others intimately, or more often, we can't bear to be known ourselves. So we stick to our PowerPoints and glossy brochures.

How, then, do we raise children who are free to love in this way, who can realize their potential for mutuality and self-giving love? Can we broken parents hope to find this freedom ourselves? God left us plenty of clues about how this freedom to love unfolds. They are written in our bodies.

Shaping Our Child's Capacity to Love

Here's one clue to resolving this conundrum: The strength of our child's connection to us shapes his capacity to love. Over time, through repeated interactions with us, our child develops an internal working model for all of his relationships. He learns what to expect from other people when he is emotionally or physically vulnerable. These expectations impact the quality of our child's relationship not only with us, his siblings, and his friends, but also with God.[2] What I'm talking about here is a process of developmental attachment that occurs in every single child whether his parents are aware of it or not.

Scientists have identified in numerous studies the critical importance of a child's *secure* attachment to her parents (especially to Mommy in the early years). In fact, it's among the most robust predictors of a child's positive psychological outcome later in life. There are four primary functions of attachment that help us understand why securely attached children do so much better in life than less secure children.[3] Secure attachment (1) provides a child with a sense of *safety*; (2) encourages the child's *internal regulation* of her emotions and impulses; (3) establishes *attunement* between the child and the parent; and (4) provides a *secure base* from which the child can explore the larger world with confidence.

Safety: A child can have longings, needs, and fears that seem strange to us, but to that child they are very real. When we respond to her with sensitivity and consistency, over time she'll feel emotionally and physically safe in our care. For infants, this means responding to their cues for comfort and food promptly, with a soothing voice and demeanor. For older children, this means helping them deal with their fears and responding to their legitimate need for mentoring, support, and encouragement. When we respond with this kind of sensitivity, our child comes to understand that her discomforts and concerns matter, that her body and opinions matter. She learns she's safe, and she trusts her parents to keep her that way.

Attunement: Have you ever had the uncomfortable experience of watching a stranger or relative misread your child's cues? They might talk too loudly, poke your child too hard ("tickling"), or toss him up in the air when he's frightened. They don't recognize your child's cues about what he needs or likes. The stranger or relative is not in sync with or attuned to your child. When we're attuned to another person, we have the ability to pick up on nuances in his behavior and subtle changes in his voice and body language in a way that shows we understand him. Without attunement we tend to project our own feelings and experiences onto the other person.

When we're attuned to our child, we understand what our

child is trying to tell us even when he's preverbal. Through small but vital exchanges with him, we learn to read his cues. In fact, we become experts in understanding those cues. Nobody knows our child like we do. Then something beautiful occurs. Encouraged by our responsiveness, our child gets better at communicating his needs and feelings. He even gets a self-confidence boost, because he "feels felt." His needs, emotions, and experiences have been recognized and respected, so he feels more comfortable in his own mind and skin.[4] When a parent is attuned to a child as he gets older, the child and parent become mutually responsive to each other's cues. The parent learns to read the child's emotions and comes to know what he needs quite naturally; the child learns how to communicate these needs and feelings because he trusts he'll be cared for. This is an empathic relationship at its best. The child and his parent are both at peace in the relationship.

Once this synchrony is established, moments of disconnection between parent and child aren't the end of the world. When securely attached children experience a mismatch between what they need and how their parents respond — perhaps because the parents are busy caring for siblings — these kids are disappointed or frustrated, but once the parent "comes back" to the child emotionally, he feels comfortable and satisfied. Older children need the challenge of this kind of delayed gratification for their healthy development.

Internal Regulation: Babies, toddlers, and most young children lack the ability to regulate their emotions. When they are faced with disappointment, resistance, or the need to delay gratification, few of them can manage it well. They experience a physiological response: Their respiration increases, their heart rate quickens, and they have a hard time thinking straight. Young children need an adult's comfort and modeling to help them calm down and come to their senses, quite literally![5] They are simply too immature to handle these moments of distress on their own. Their options are to explode (temper tantrum) or shut down (withdrawal or depression). When infants and children are helped through their experiences of emotional distress by a calm and understanding parent, over time they learn how to get through them alone. This is self-regulation. Through repeated experiences of being comforted and calmed, the child internalizes these strategies and begins to do it himself. This leads to a sense of competence and increased self-esteem.[6]

Secure Base for Exploration: How well we nurture our young children influences their later vitality, curiosity, and intrinsic sense of self. God created our children with a desire to explore and learn about the world, but they're also born completely helpless and dependent on us to meet their needs for food, comfort, and safety. From the age of one year onward, the quality of a child's attachment to her primary caregiver creates her "base" for exploration. If she is secure in this base, she'll be motivated to venture forth to explore and discover her world through play and creative solitude. This sense of security also gives her confidence and competence as she approaches increasingly difficult developmental tasks.[7]

Many parents face finger-wagging about spoiling their babies and toddlers; they're told that if they want their children to become autonomous and independent, then they need to let the child get used to being alone and self-soothing. There are two problems with this proposition. First, the end of human maturation is not independence, but rather *interdependence*. Only truly independent, autonomous people can form healthy interdependent relationships in which both parties give and receive love and anticipate and meet each other's needs. Second, how do children arrive at independence? *Attachment*, rather than separation, is the vehicle through which our children become independent.[8] *Attachment*, not separation, creates the womb of maturation. When our children are exposed to more separation than they can bear in childhood, they become *less* independent: They become fixated on substitute attachments, or they become stuck in self-numbing behaviors. When our children are attached to us, they feel a secure base in the relationship, and this gives them the power to burst forth and chart their course in life. First, they need that secure base beneath them.

Parents continue to be a child's secure base into the teen years and even beyond. The support our children need is less physical as they get older, but they still need a safe haven from the storms of life. As they move away from us toward psychological and even physical independence, they will occasionally "check in" with us emotionally. I have a young adult son. Although he is well on his way to adulthood, he still turns to my husband and me for reassurance during important transitions in his life (such as when he traveled alone for the first time and when he left for college). Then, before we know it, he's off again on his path of discovery.

So, whether they are exploring some blocks across the room as toddlers, having their first sleepover at school age, or exploring whether to become a religious sister or a doctor as a teenager, our children are more willing to reach beyond themselves to something bigger when their hunger for attachment is satiated. Secure children have a great zest for life and the ability to recover from small setbacks because they have a safe haven in their parents' hearts and arms. Attachment gives our children an abiding and enduring sense that they belong with us, that they are safe with us, and that they matter.

Attachment Gives Us the Power to Parent

A child's attachment to his parents is the key factor that makes it possible for them to guide him and for him to recognize them as his best bet for getting his needs met.[9] A child will naturally resist a person's lead, pressure, or directions if he's not attached to that person. This is a built-in defense to protect him from outsiders, but if this defense is triggered with his parents, it works against the parent-child relationship and the wellbeing of the child. One of the most important benefits of a child's secure attachment is that it makes us endearing to him, and it makes him want to follow, look up to, and take his cues from us. Attachment allows us to become the compass for our children, transmitting our culture and values to them, guiding their behavior, keeping them safe, and leading them toward wholeness. As I'll explore in later chapters, without a deep attachment to us our children pick up their culture and values from substitute attachments (such as peers or celebrities), and we have to resort to gimmicks, threats, and increasingly distorted techniques to handle their resistance to our parenting.

When Attachment Fails

When a parent is unpredictable, emotionally distant, or scary, a child is forced to adapt her behaviors to deal with her natural fear of separation or abandonment. These behaviors are self-protective in nature. They are defenses against a pain that's too much for a child to bear: a parent's rejection, instability, or abuse. They help the child tolerate or block out the wounding, but in the long run they can become toxic and may prevent the child from forming healthy relationships. The child internalizes the "rules" she learns through her interactions with her early caregivers; she then tends to apply these rules to all her relationships in childhood and even into adulthood, unless new experiences help her repair that early wounding.

Insecure attachment tends to organize into one of three relational patterns depending on the parent's actions, responses, and demeanor. These three patterns are (1) Anxious-Insecure, (2) Avoidant-Insecure, and (3) Disorganized-Insecure. These patterns reflect the child's basic assumptions or core beliefs about herself and others, and those assumptions become a lens through which she filters her experiences in relationships.[10]

Anxious-Insecure

Parents of anxious-insecure children are inconsistent or unpredictable with their love. At times the parents are kind, responsive, and caring, but at other times they are emotionally unavailable or very intrusive. For example, the parent may ignore the child entirely one day, and then overwhelm the child with attention and affection the next day. Because the child doesn't know what to expect, he becomes preoccupied with his parent's behavior and moods, sometimes to the exclusion of other healthy childhood interests like playing and exploring. A role reversal may emerge in which the child feels he needs to take care of the parent, either physically or emotionally.

These kids tend to develop the following patterns:

- They become overwhelmed by separations from the parent, but when the parent returns they can seem both clingy and angry.
- They are anxious in new situations.
- As they mature, they have a negative view of themselves and a positive view of others.
- They are vulnerable to bullying.
- Older children have difficulty sustaining friendships and functioning in peer groups. They want to create a sense of closeness so desperately that they tend to share too much of themselves too early and they smother people with their neediness.
- They dread abandonment, so they may stay in unhealthy relationships.

Avoidant-Insecure

Parents of these kids tend to be cold, harsh, or rejecting. They ignore or dismiss the child's cues of distress when he's hurt or sick. They often view crying as a form of manipulation, so they ignore it, even in infants. Well-meaning parents of avoidant children may try to meet the child's needs on the parents' terms — often on a strict schedule that has little to do with the child's physical or emotional needs at the moment. In exchange for having one of their attachment needs met (physical proximity), these children learn to shut down their other needs.

Avoidant-insecure children tend to struggle in the following ways:

- They are emotionally distant. Babies and toddlers seem not to care much when their parent leaves or returns. They may be called "good babies" because they don't fuss much, but their lack of interest in their parents is a defense.
- They seem prematurely independent and self-sufficient.
- As they mature, they have a positive view of themselves and a negative view of others.
- They may bully other children.
- They are angry, aggressive, and defiant toward their parents or other children.
- They are extremely sensitive to negative evaluation.
- When in emotional pain, they withdraw rather than reach out for help.
- Teenagers have few friends and these friendships tend to be isolated and marked by jealousy. They are not very involved with their families.

Disorganized-Insecure

This is the most troubling attachment category. Parents of the disorganized-insecure child scare the child. The parent might behave in bizarre, unpredictable ways while under the influence of drugs or alcohol, or even physically and emotionally abuse the child, exploding in a rage in response to small triggers. A child of these parents faces a dilemma: one part of his brain wants to run away from the thing that frightens him, but another part of his brain can't tolerate separation from his attachment figure. These children are emotionally stuck, and many will develop disorganized attachment.

Disorganized attachment is expressed in the following ways:

- Infants display chaotic responses to the parents — they seek the parents and then reject them.
- They have a negative view of both themselves and others.
- Like avoidant children, they don't believe others are reliable or accessible; like anxious children, they don't believe they deserve to be loved.
- They are controlling of their parents and aggressive toward their peers.
- School-age children may have impaired academic abilities.
- They learn to disassociate as a coping mechanism.

Of course, attachment is a continuum. Some children are pretty secure but may exhibit some insecure attachment behaviors, perhaps with particular persons or during crises. It's important to note, too, that children come to us with different temperaments; some children just don't like to be held much and aren't particularly talkative. Kids are different, and they do better when we allow space for these differences. But insecure attachment is not shaped by temperament; it is shaped by relationship experiences. Your child's temperament will not make her insecure, chaotic, withdrawn, or depressed.

Every Catholic parent should pay attention to attachment. The principle of the common good in Catholic social doctrine tells us that we are to order our homes for the common good of all persons in our families.[11] The common good includes anything that allows our children to reach "their own fulfillment"[12] more fully and more easily, anything that fulfills the needs of the "body and soul."[13] We can debate many things about what children need in order to reach their potential, but attachment is not one of them. All children have a right to a secure attachment because it's essential to their flourishing; it's part of the unfolding of a child's capacity for self-giving love, peace, and deep faith.

Attachment Science v. "Attachment Parenting"

In my discussion of childhood attachment, I haven't said anything about the practices commonly associated with the parenting style known as "attachment parenting," such as baby-wearing, cosleeping, and breastfeeding. I am a big advocate of all these practices. They made my life easier — not harder — when my children were infants. However, I won't emphasize these practices here, because, as Dr. William Sears puts it, they are "tools not rules."[14] But a reliable, emotionally sensitive, trusting connection between parent and child is a rule, not a tool, because without it children will never mature to their potential. Furthermore, attachment is relevant not only in our relationships with our infants, but also with our older children. In fact, attachment is relevant to all human relationships, including those among adults. It's the most powerful factor in human maturation and our ability to give and receive love.

The Six Phases of Attachment

The first few years of a child's life are critical to his healthy emotional development. In fact, a baby's brain is more vulnerable to environmental influences during the first months following birth than at any other time in his life.[15] However, parents are sometimes led to believe that the human capacity for relationship is imprinted on the baby and, boom, they're set for life. Quite the contrary, it takes many years to fully realize, and only if conditions are right. Dr. Gordon Neufeld has proposed a six-phase attachment paradigm that is useful for understanding this process,[16] ascending from the simplest way of attaching to the most complex. The phases are:

1. **Proximity** — seeking physical closeness through the five senses
2. **Sameness** — imitating the other person or sharing the same interests
3. **Belonging** — loyalty even during conflict
4. **Significance** — feeling important to the other person
5. **Love** — emotional intimacy; giving our hearts away
6. **Being known** — psychological intimacy; sharing our true selves

Each phase builds on the previous one, deepening the roots of the connection. Each succeeding phase of attaching becomes the answer to the separation (or fear of separation) experienced in the previous phase. So, for example, when our child can draw close to us through sameness, he's better able to bear the anxiety experienced when he can't be physically close to us, maybe because he's beginning to walk. When he realizes he isn't exactly the same as us, this is alarming for him, but when he's able to see himself as part of our family, or he senses we're on the same side, it softens this separation. And so on.

All human relationships follow this pattern of attachment, and for the relationship to be secure and enduring, they must do so. Sometimes a relationship is weakened when one of these attachment needs is neglected or ignored. So I might enjoy physical closeness with my spouse (proximity), and we may both be Catholic and love the opera (sameness), but if I don't feel very special to him, or if I question his loyalty to me, I won't feel loved or deeply known by him. I won't give my heart away, because the attachment is weak.

If all goes well, a child can move through the six phases with his primary attachment figure one phase at a time in the first six years of life, so that by age six or seven the child becomes securely attached. Note, however, that arriving at secure attachment by age six is *possible*, but not *inevitable*. Many of us never reach the later phases of attachment. (But it's never too late for our attachment potential to be realized.[17] Challenging, yes, but never too late.) So, even in ideal circumstances, if Neufeld is right, infants are incapable of deep, enduring attachment. They can have their attachment need for proximity met, but they have more attachment maturing to do. Little babies are sensory beings, and they do best with a lot of consistent, close physical contact with their parents, which is why I encourage the use of baby-bonding tools. However, after she comes to trust that her need for physical proximity will be met, the child continues to need her parents to gather her to them in sameness, loyalty, significance, and love, until finally she feels deeply known. There's one hunger for connection but six ways of attaching. If development is healthy, "the six strands become interwoven into a strong rope of connection that can preserve closeness even under the most adverse circumstances."[18] Note that the "phases" are also modes: Once the child becomes capable of connecting in proximity, sameness, or significance, and so on, the parent can connect with the child in each of these modes. A child who has reached his attachment potential can connect in all six modes, though he may prefer one mode to another at different times.

When a chronic attachment deficit occurs in a parent-child relationship, the child will build up defenses, and an attachment disorder may result, as described above. A child can become stuck in the early phases of attachment or try to force later stages in an inauthentic way. For example, an anxiously attached middle schooler in a desperate yearning for emotional intimacy will share too much of herself too soon in friendships, which pushes the friend away. Of course, disconnection in one of the six areas can occur even in very healthy relationships, even between a parent and child with secure attachment. I'm talking about a chronic attachment issue that creates dysfunction in the child's relationships. If you're concerned about an attachment deficit or even a temporary disconnect, you can fill your child's "attachment cup" through one or all of these six modes of connecting.

The Six Phases in Real Life

Neufeld's attachment model has made a significant contribution to attachment theory, and what's great for us is that it's pretty easy for any parent to understand. I first encountered it in 2006 when my children were still very young. Over the years, it has given me direction and confidence in my parenting. I understood attachment conceptually, but after the infant phase, I was a little unsure what my kids needed from me other than my warmth and sensitivity. Recognizing the six ways of attaching helped me understand what to look for in the first six years and how to connect with my kids depending on which mode they were in when they were seeking closeness to me. It was an epiphany that kids don't draw close to us only through cuddles and kisses.

The model also gave me concrete ideas for gathering my children emotionally, no matter their ages. If your child is age six or younger, you might find Deborah MacNamara's *Rest, Play, Grow: Making Sense of Preschoolers* helpful as you navigate the six phases with your small kids. MacNamara is one of Neufeld's former students, and she does a marvelous job of explaining how to lead very young children to a deep connection with their parents. For older kids, I have some practical suggestions:

Proximity: How can you draw physically closer to your child? Build a tent in the backyard and sleep in it overnight. Or play a card or board game. Recently my husband and my teenage daughter, Claire, decided to embark on a fitness routine together. They go on hikes and do a dance program on our game console. These are fun and nonthreatening ways to enjoy physical proximity! Chapter 3 of this book offers more ideas for building playful rapport with your child, and most require physical proximity. This mode includes all the senses, so singing to and with, and cooking for and with, your children are two more great ways to connect.

Sameness: Look for things you have in common with your child and point them out. If you think about it, you'll realize how many interests you share. Think of something you might explore together or talk about. Technology? Music? Sports? Baking? Good jokes? My oldest son, Aidan, and I both enjoy talking about philosophy and politics. As he's matured, our conversations have become challenging and fascinating! I love it when he sends me articles or shares a book he's reading. Of course, our shared faith is the most important "sameness" in our families. In chapter 6, I offer some ideas for building a strong Catholic culture in your home, which can deepen even further your shared identity in our Faith.

Belonging and Loyalty: When your child is having a tough day, let her know you're on her side, even if you disagree with a choice she's made. Listen without lecturing. If there's a lesson you want to teach because she's made a poor decision, empathize first ("Wow, that sounds awful. That must have really hurt your feelings"). Once she knows you understand her perspective, you can share your own. For me, this often means I look for the good intention behind my child's choice. When you have a conflict with her, ensure your child knows you're still on her side, and that the two of you will work it out together. Never embarrass her in front of friends or family. This is particularly important with teenagers.

Significance: Children yearn to know how special they are to us. Tell your child the story of her birth and how much she changed your life when she was born. Proudly hang up her art projects, read her poems aloud at the dinner table, or take the whole family out for ice cream when she graduates from elementary school. Tuck notes in her lunch box, or pick up her favorite chocolate for no particular reason. Point out all the ways she makes the world more interesting and enjoyable. One of the most important ways we make our kids feel significant is by prioritizing our family life and their needs.

Love: This is emotional intimacy, and it requires great vulnerability. Emotional intimacy is about revealing our emotional stirrings and struggles with somebody we trust. We can't be emotionally vulnerable when we fear we'll be rejected or judged, so from her earliest years through to adulthood, be a safe harbor for your child's heart. In the discipline and empathy chapters, I'll explain how important it is to allow a child to have all her feelings, even the ones that make us uncomfortable, such as anger and sadness. While we can guide her in expressing her emotions appropriately, we want to invite her to be honest about all her emotions so she can live with vitality.

Being Known: Here we arrive at psychological intimacy, which is about being "real" with somebody. We all long to be deeply known. When you feel deeply known by someone, you feel comfortable sharing your honest opinions, quirky ideas, and even mistakes with her. You can reveal your vulnerability because you know your heart is safe. With children, this stage often emerges when they realize they have their own thoughts and they don't have to tell you about them. They draw closer to you by telling their "secrets." We encourage and protect this phase by being approachable and accepting our children, even when they mess up. Two guidelines here are trying to see the positive intention behind a poor choice and honoring your child's unique gifts even if you don't possess those gifts.

You can use these six areas of connection to strengthen and deepen your child's attachment to you. I've found the way they play out is very different depending on the context and the child. Sometimes a child makes it clear that she needs to connect in one particular mode, but at other times you have to do the work and touch on all the modes. So, maybe in one conversation with a weepy teenager whose friend didn't invite her to a party, you offer a cuddle (proximity), and then, while she's venting her anger or frustration (emotional intimacy), you make her favorite tea (significance) which you keep on hand just for moments like this. You assure her, "I would feel the same as you" (sameness) and "No matter what, I'm on your side" (loyalty). You allow her to share her real thoughts without judgment (psychological intimacy). This is running the ladder of attachment. I've discovered that even after our children become capable of higher modes of attaching that require more maturity and vulnerability, sometimes they need to connect to us through the simpler modes for different reasons, perhaps in a crisis or when returning home after being away. Even we grown-ups do this with our spouses: Sometimes we just want to be held. When my college son comes home from college on a break, he likes me to feed him (five senses/proximity), and he wants to watch some of the old movies we enjoyed together as a family when he was little (sameness).

Attachment and Spiritual Development

As Catholics, we know that no model of human flourishing is complete if it leaves out a consideration of the transcendent.[19] Why is this hunger for attachment and deep connection there within us at all, especially our complex longing for psychological and emotional intimacy? I think the attachment phases are really homing devices. These yearnings play a role in our transformation and growth in holiness. The Church reminds us, "The desire for God is written in the human heart, because man is created by God and for God; and God never ceases to draw man to himself" (CCC 27). Consider for a moment our desire to be deeply known. Only our Creator can know us completely and perfectly, but the imperfect intimacy we experience in relationships here on earth prepares us for and draws us closer toward that Perfect Intimacy. When we offer our fiat, we experience the self-transcendence and openness to truth that allows for great fulfillment while we're still on earth.[20]

What happens if we're moving through life with deep attachment wounds, but trying to connect to God? When I first became interested in attachment science, I don't recall the existence of any studies exploring how a person's attachment status influenced her relationship with the ultimate attachment figure: God. However, in the last fifteen years, more research has emerged that shows a correlation between childhood attachment and later faith development and spiritual growth. **Securely attached** young adults have religious standards (beliefs and practices) that tend to correspond to those of their parents. So if the family was religious, they tend to continue participating in their faith in young adulthood. If the family was irreligious, they tend not to be particularly religious.

In contrast, **insecurely attached** young adults are more likely to distance themselves from the religiosity of their parents, whatever that might look like, in an effort to find emotional equilibrium.[21] For those of us concerned about transmitting our Catholic faith to our children, we can't afford to ignore these observations. While it's a natural part of faith development to have doubts and questions about what we've been taught about God as little kids (more about this in chapter 6), securely attached young adults seem to be able to move through this stage with greater grace. Even if they have doubts, they have confidence that they'll find answers and that the people they love will support them through it. This allows them to move on to a more mature stage of faith where they're able to accept the inevitable paradoxes and mysteries of faith.

A child's attachment status also influences his later spiritual development (as distinguished from his religious beliefs and practices). Research[22] shows that **securely attached** children who grow up in a home with clear religious values will tend to experience God as open, loving, and fair. They'll be capable of a deepening prayer life and an evolving sense of their personal mission within Christ's Church. Because of this, they may traverse the path of spiritual growth and discipleship more comfortably than insecurely attached children.

Not surprisingly, **anxiously attached** children grow up feeling like they must work hard to win God's approval. They doubt their value in God's eyes. As adults, they tend to emphasize religious form (kneeling correctly, following rules) over spiritual growth. They might attend church, but mostly out of a sense of duty rather than love for Christ or the Church he established. They'll avoid being honest with God about their disappointment in or anger with him. However, like in their human relationships, these negative feelings will fester beneath the surface. Eventually, they may feel abandoned by God. At this point, they'll either continue attending church while feeling estranged from God, or they'll leave the Faith behind and go about their lives trying to fill their emptiness with counterfeit forms of love.

Kids with **avoidant attachment** learn early that they can't depend on anybody. So in their relationship with God, they don't see the point of reaching out. As adults, they value prestige and the admiration of others, so if they're active in a church, it's usually because there's some personal benefit to them. They don't really care about building a community, let alone developing a close bond with God.

Adults with insecure attachment may attend church, but their spiritual growth tends to flatline at an immature stage. They're there for the friendships and the social benefits, or because their spouse wants them to go. Can these people become disciples of Christ? Can they move away from that crowd at the back of the room toward Christ, to experience him as a friend who loves them and has a special mission for them? Of course! God's providence can transform their sufferings, and they can become great witnesses of God's mercy and tenderness. But it's a difficult battle. Most spiritual directors advise a person who carries unresolved childhood pain, including attachment issues, to seek psychological counseling either before or during spiritual direction. Even Saint Ignatius of

Loyola declined to direct Saint Peter Faber (cofounder of the Society of Jesus) in the Spiritual Exercises when they first met, because Peter was terrified of God and was obsessively scrupulous. Peter had to wait four years before Ignatius believed he was ready.[23]

What can we learn from this as we seek to raise children who are prepared for discipleship? It makes many parents uncomfortable, but the evidence is mounting that our relationship with our children — how warm, accepting, supportive, and responsive we are — creates the lens through which our children experience and approach their relationship with God later on. In many ways, this is our purpose as parents: We create the picture in our children's minds about what God is like.

In her important book on adult discipleship, *Forming Intentional Disciples*, Sherry Weddell describes five "thresholds" or stages of conversion as people move toward real discipleship. (The thresholds are focused on one's lived relationship with God, not one's religious practices.) The first threshold, which a person needs to move through in order to embark on the path of discipleship, is "initial trust": "A person is able to *trust* or has a positive association with Jesus Christ, the Church, a Christian believer, or something identifiably Christian. Trust is *not* the same as active personal faith. Without some kind of bridge of trust in place, people will not move closer to God."[24]

Without question, parents are the bridge of trust par excellence for their children. That first relationship makes it easier or harder for the child later to trust others and God as he seeks a deeper faith life. That first relationship also makes it easier or harder to be free to love other seekers with a disciple's heart. A person with secure attachment is far more likely to practice both agape (self-giving love) and philia (we-giving love). His heart is open and ready for authentic encounter in a community of faith.

Conversion requires us to get outside our own heads. We have to be able to listen and trust. People with attachment issues are so locked inside themselves that they can hardly have a conversation without obsessing about what they look or sound like. If you can't release yourself to the experience of conversation and friendship, you will never be drawn into discipleship. You will resist the agape and philia in others, and you will never extend it yourself.

Of course, we can't force our children to become disciples. Even if they have a capacity for a relationship with Jesus, they have to take that step. Through the generosity of our love, we can prepare our children to reach the bridge to discipleship, but they have to make the choice to cross it. They have to cultivate the life of prayer that's necessary in a growing relationship with God. But if we fulfill our parts as well as we can, at least they'll be ready!

When Parents Aren't Free to Love

If secure attachment is among the most reliable predictors of your child's optimal well-being later in life, then what's the most reliable predictor of your child's secure attachment? It's not whether you babywear, stay at home with your kids, or even read the right parenting books. *It's your own adult attachment status.*[25] If I ask you whether you're attached to your child, you'll most likely respond with a confident yes, because you love him so intensely. But feeling love for your child is very different from possessing the freedom to respond to his need for physical closeness, emotional availability, and sensitivity. We can acquire plenty of head knowledge about what kids need to thrive, but if we lack self-awareness about why we feel more or less comfortable with connection to others, we may find ourselves doing things that undermine our hopes of raising healthy children who are emotionally prepared for a life of Christian discipleship.

Sometimes we experience emotional roadblocks (or landmines) with our kids that seem to arise from nowhere, without warning. We ignore, scream at, or even hit our kids despite making a conscious decision not to do these things. We hurt them, and we know it. We recall that day they were born, when we planned to give them the very best of ourselves, but here they are witnessing the worst in us. We imagined we would be caring, fun-loving, inspiring parents, but at times like this we feel like merely tolerable parents. Where is this coming from? Just like children, adults develop internal mechanisms for coping with emotional disequilibrium. Because of this, unhealthy habits of relating to our kids can seep into our parenting.

It goes without saying that not every parent who "behaves badly" has some kind of deep attachment problem. Some of us struggle with impatience, anger, or pride, and we need to work on developing greater virtue. Others of us notice that one or two behaviors in our kids seem to touch a nerve and we become reactive, so we need to gain awareness about these sensitivities. However, although any parent can have problems with emotional regulation or overreacting at some point, for some of us, understanding adult attachment will help us make better sense of our lives and fill in a few pieces of a puzzle we can't seem to solve.

Scientists have identified the dominant attachment patterns in adults and how these patterns tend to influence parenting behavior:[26] **Secure** adults are capable of experiencing a wide range of feelings. They feel comfortable in intimate relationships. They believe they can count on others, and they don't mind when others depend on them for support. They have a balanced view of their own parents: They acknowledge that their parents made some mistakes, but they have made peace with this reality. After working through any residue of childhood pain, either through significant adult relationships or professional counseling, they have a generally positive feeling about their childhoods and themselves. When they become parents, they're able to meet their child's needs with warmth and consistency, and they bounce back quickly from bad days with their kids.

Preoccupied adults may have been anxiously attached children. They have a positive view of others, but a negative view of themselves. They're very self-critical, seeking frequent affirmation from others, but nobody can say anything to take away their deep-seated self-doubts. They're very preoccupied with their relationships — worrying, planning, evaluating. They tend to be impulsive, and they're often the pursuers in romantic relationships. They try to avoid displays of anger for fear of rejection, but their anger simmers and sometimes they explode. They may feel jealous when their spouse, friends, or even their children want to spend time with somebody other than them.

Preoccupied parents may invade their child's space, either emotionally or physically. They tend to seek connection in ways that reveal a lack of empathy. They mistake their own emotional neediness for love and end up being intrusive and insensitive. They may depend inappropriately on their children to affirm their own value, so the child feels responsible for the parent's well-being. They risk doing things that cause their child to develop anxious-attachment behaviors.

Dismissive adults are loner types. They may have developed avoidant attachment as a child. They seem arrogant; they have a high opinion of themselves and a low opinion of others (including their spouses). They lack empathy, often failing to perceive the emotional experiences of others or to understand nonverbal cues. They tend to carry an extreme view of their parents, describing their parents with language that either idealizes or vilifies them. Yet they're uncomfortable talking about their childhoods and have difficulty recalling details about what happened to them in their homes. As a defense mechanism, dismissive adults tell themselves they don't need close relationships. They reject others before they can be rejected. They preempt firings and romantic breakups by ending the relationships first.

Dismissive adults love their kids, but the normal neediness and demands of children can irritate them because they've rejected any sign of these qualities in themselves. They encourage premature independence in the child, so that the child ends up feeling less capable. When their children are clingy or whiny, they may react with anger and frustration. Their responses to their child's needs tend to be out of proportion to the signals the child is giving. These parents also focus on their child's external achievement because this is how they measure their own value. The child can feel they are only acceptable and lovable when they achieve the highest accolades. Dismissive adults risk raising avoidant children.

Now, this is not a recipe we're talking about. Dismissive adults won't always raise avoidant children, and preoccupied adults won't always raise anxiously attached children. Adult attachment status is a risk factor, but protective factors in a child's life — such as having other secure adults around, having a stable home, having a positive disposition, and even having enjoyable hobbies — can buffer the effect of living with a parent who has an attachment issue. Prayer is the best protective factor: Pray with and for your children.

Parenting tends to draw our brokenness to the surface, where we can face it. It can bring us to a point where we finally understand many things about our relationships. This has been very true for me. I was almost certainly an anxiously attached child who became a preoccupied adult. By the mercy of God, I knew this before I had my first baby. When I was a young woman, I was successful academically, and I appeared to have it together on the exterior, but because of some childhood trauma I suffered from severe anxiety and self-doubt. I struggled with transparency and vulnerability in all my relationships; it was very easy to isolate myself behind my external success. I felt anchorless and lonely. I was fortunate to live near renowned trauma specialist Dr. Bessel Van Der Kolk, who treated me for post-traumatic stress disorder. His work draws on attachment theory, which immediately intrigued me, because I had learned some years before that one of my parents had been diagnosed with an attachment disorder during a divorce proceeding.

I read everything I could about attachment theory, and while I had access to many other explanations for my suffering, nothing made as much sense to me as the exquisite drama of human attachment. I discovered that attachment is the single most significant factor in our innate drive to become a separate, viable human being, which in turn allows us to hold on to our sense of self while experiencing togetherness. If we're emotionally healthy, we can hold on to those we love while becoming our true selves. I've continued to learn about attachment for nearly twenty-five years, and I still don't know very much. But understanding even a little about the process of attachment in the maturing process has helped me make better sense of myself and my children.

My hope is that it will provide you with a few insights too. Even if you don't struggle with attachment, most of us have some kind of healing to do, and parenting, like few other experiences, can make this abundantly clear.

Becoming a Resurrection Parent

The good news is that it's entirely possible to give our children what we don't have ourselves, and sometimes in giving it to them, we find our own healing. When you recognize you have some kind of limitation, you have taken the first step. With a little insight, you'll begin to understand why in certain exchanges with your children, you say or do things you regret later. For those of us with deep wounds, we tend to respond like this because we're *reacting* subconsciously to unresolved experiences from our past rather than *responding* freely to the situations in front of us. Our perceptions and even unconscious memories shape our responses to everyday situations in which we're called upon to respond to our children's cues for comfort, support, or love.[27] Basically, we're being controlled by emotions from the past that have nothing to do with our children.

All parents, even those with a secure adult attachment status, might yell at, scare, or hit their kids even after they've made a decision not to do these things. These parents may never have learned how to cope with frustration and intense emotion when they were little. In fact, they may have been shamed for expressing any negative emotions, so they think having negative emotions with their children now is a sign of sin or weakness. As I'll explain in chapter 5, we all need to learn to live with hard emotions such as anger and frustration, so we can move through them to the other side of them. This is the only way to become a mature, integrated adult. When we experience hard emotions, the key to civilized behavior is not in some superhuman personal resolve or avoiding our feelings. We have to make room for our angry, frustrated emotions so that our brains can find better answers to the emotions than our impulses to yell and hit. We have to identify our mixed feelings ("I want to yell, but it's not the right answer") so we can find another way to release that intense rush of adrenaline.[28] We develop patience not by pretending we're not frustrated, but by experiencing frustration and finding appropriate answers to it, answers that protect our children and preserve our connection to them. This is real virtue.

After we gain this awareness, we can develop strategies for dealing with those moments when we tend to react rather than respond to our children. Here are some practical tips.

Understand Your Freak-Out Threshold

All of us have a point at which we can no longer think rationally, and, at this point, we'll fail to experience the mixed feelings I just described. The mixed feelings are what give us pause before we act or speak, so that our higher, rational brain can help us make wise decisions. If we don't have access to these mixed feelings, we'll tend to act or speak impulsively. We all have a different limit for what we can handle before we reach this point of no return. I call this my "freak-out threshold." After I reach my threshold, I'm no longer tuned into the people around me; I'm shut down and in flight-or-fight mode. I have no interest in what some author recommends I do during conflict; I just criticize, huff around, blame, or yell. We want to remain on the high road where we can make wise choices in our relationship with our kids. You learn what your freak-out threshold is by paying attention to how your emotional temperature rises or falls.[29] Most of the time you're probably feeling pretty mellow and engaged with your kids. But pay attention to what happens when some stress is added to the mix; for example, when you're trying to get out the door in the morning or dealing with several kids with competing needs. You may still be in control, but you begin to feel the tension below the surface. It's a lot harder at this point to maintain your composure, but you're still capable of making rational decisions and engaging politely and rationally with the people around you. It's very important that you recognize when you're moving beyond this threshold. After this point, you'll find it much harder to manage your stress without an attacking-type energy (yelling, blaming, threatening). If we go beyond our personal threshold, we're no longer in control, and we'll probably say things we later regret.

Your threshold will change day to day depending on many factors. If you're like most people, specific triggers can cause you to ramp up more easily mentally or emotionally, so that you reach your freak-out threshold very quickly. These triggers create what I call a "spark point" — an immediate negative reaction that comes from some deep place within us. They have nothing to do with the person we're talking to. Some triggers don't create immediate reactions, but they can also just eat at us slowly or wear us down. Some of us are more sensitive to some stressors, but not others. I know people who are pretty much unfazed by fifty people showing up at their house for dinner, but they become overwhelmed quickly by the ordinary needs of their small children. I know others who thrive happily with eight to twelve kids in tow, but if a grocery store clerk is rude to them, they will curse at the clerk. When we pass our threshold, we lose our filters and we will fail to act with virtue. So it's imperative that we're honest with ourselves about how we're put together for the sake of our children (and grocery store clerks).

Many parents struggle with sleep deprivation, overscheduling, or illness. These stressors leave us physically drained, so we have a harder time drawing on our more mature, rational resources. This is true of me. When I haven't had enough sleep for several days in a row, my threshold drops, and I seem to snap at my kids more easily. Your triggers might also be particular behaviors in your kids: clinginess, whining, demands, shrieking, or tantrums. You might notice particular transitions in your day put you on edge: bedtime, getting out the door for Mass, afternoon homework.

Reflect on how you respond to these triggers emotionally. Your mind might start chattering away in anger, frustration, or self-doubt. You might find yourself becoming emotionally rigid or chaotic. You might notice yourself ruminating on what you're going to do to your child if he doesn't "knock it off." If left to yourself, you know that eventually you may say or do something you'll later regret.[30] This is all about gaining a simple awareness of our stress levels before it's too late and we're on the low road toward what is essentially an adult temper tantrum. Changing our behaviors starts with recognizing these kinds of patterns.

Create Your Battle Plan

After you identify your freak-out threshold and your triggers, have a concrete plan for what you will do in situations in which you know you're headed in the wrong direction emotionally. I honestly think this is a spiritual battle we're talking about, so it requires a battle plan. The love between a parent and child is one of the most powerful forces for good in the world. The devil is prepared to do whatever it takes to undermine it. He knows well our fears and blind spots, and he uses them to his own advantage. But we can defeat him. We can make a decision when we're clear-headed about how we'll handle ourselves during a trigger encounter with a child. You need a release or outlet. What will help you get your stress down to a manageable level? Will you call your spouse or a trusted friend? Will you take your child for a walk or put on some music? I've noticed that sometimes just changing my physical position helps me reverse course. If I'm standing up, I sit down; if I'm sitting down, I stand up and walk around. Doing this seems to reverse the direction of emotions so that my higher brain can take over. Often the best thing we can do is take a break. In the next chapter, I share how I used to have an afternoon family nap hour every day so I could refuel and collect my thoughts. Perhaps you can do something similar when you need to get a handle on your emotional temperature.

Lean on God

God won't refuse us if we ask the Holy Spirit to come to our aid! When I'm headed down the low road, I find great comfort in the prayer to Mary, Undoer of Knots. It's been offered by many souls facing difficult, even hopeless, situations. You will find the prayer at the end of this chapter. I have a treasured Mary, Undoer of Knots prayer card with an image of the famous Schmidtner painting showing the Virgin Mary untying ribbons. (Jorge Mario Bergoglio — later Pope Francis — encouraged a devotion to Mary, Undoer of Knots in Argentina and Brazil after coming across Schmidtner's painting in a church in Germany.) I keep this prayer card close to me. I highly recommend Marge Fenelon's guided meditation, *Our Lady, Undoer of Knots: A Living Novena*, which will help you recognize the knots in your life that need untying. When we untie these knots, our freak-out thresholds increase (we can handle more stress before we reach our limits), and we can experience peace of mind even in very challenging circumstances.

I have also found a devotion to the Rosary to be indispens-able as I confront my own limitations with my kids. It would be difficult to pray a whole Rosary in the middle of most trig-ger encounters, but maintaining a devotion to the Rosary will bring you many graces, including increased patience and for-giveness. When I started praying the Rosary regularly, I began to understand how pain and joy can coexist when we surren-der to God. The Rosary allows us to confront and offer up our old wounds. We begin to make sense of our past experiences as we view them through Christ's experiences and Mary's re-sponses to what she witnessed during her son's lifetime.

3Regular retreats are also helpful for parents; they allow us to recover from the physical and emotional demands of parenting. In the next chapter, I offer advice for creating lit-tle retreats with our children in tow. This might be just the thing to collect our wits when we're frazzled. In addition to these retreats, I think occasional personal retreats where we're alone are helpful for parents, especially for those with small children. A retreat needn't be expensive or extravagant. De-pending on our circumstances, taking a retreat might mean a weekly hour alone before the Blessed Sacrament, an afternoon in a nature reserve with a rosary, or a weekend away at a Cath-olic retreat center. The important thing is that you're able to find solitude, even if briefly.

The solitude of a retreat can be difficult for many people with adult attachment problems, but this is why they're also so healing. Securely attached adults can emotionally hold on to their loved ones even when they're apart, but insecurely attached adults struggle with this. We feel uncomfortable on retreats where we are separated from our relationship "fixes." We need constant reminders from our loved ones that we're lovable or admirable, to such a degree that we're turned in on ourselves. When we're alone on a retreat, we're cut off from these things that we're clinging to in order to feel okay, even though they are keeping us from forming mature bonds and growing spiritually. Such relationship fixations get in the way of our dependence on and faith in God. So in retreat, we're forced to come face to face with God. Over time, we're forced to come face to face with ourselves in relationship to God, including our ambivalence about or anger with him. While this is difficult, it's worth the struggle. In the long run, I found that (and this astonished me when I realized it in retrospect) when I attended to my relationship with God, my other relationships began healing. As those relationships blossomed, my relationship with God could deepen even further. And so on. It's a synergy powered by grace.

You see, we are never stuck. We do come to adulthood with a set of beliefs about how to handle anger, how lovable we are, and how trustworthy others are, but these beliefs can be revised over time through loving relationships with friends, our family, and God. They are revised when we challenge our assumptions and risk giving our hearts away. New, healthy relationships can change how you view yourself and others. You learn that others can really be trusted, you are worthy of love, and you are capable of loving with vulnerability and honesty.

God accompanies us along the way as we make these choices to change our relationship patterns. Of course, we'll never erase the truth of our past experiences. A hint of that old pain might appear on occasion. Sometimes this reality catches us by surprise and we're disappointed. Just remember, when the risen Christ appeared to his disciples, he still bore the wounds of the crucifixion. The Resurrection didn't erase the truth of the pain he had endured. His wounds were so much a part of him that he brought them with him not only to his death, but also to his risen life. His wounds bear a meaning that continues to reverberate throughout history.

This says something to us about our own sufferings: We may always bear signs of some of the wounds of the past; we cannot erase the reality that others have failed to love us well.

But God never wastes anything, not even the most nonsensical acts of cruelty. He uses it all to draw us toward others and to himself. He redeems our suffering. We become resurrection parents when we allow God to do this for us — not merely tolerable parents, but resurrection parents who live in faith, hope, and love right alongside our children.

Mary, Undoer of Knots, pray for us.
Through your grace, your intercession, and your example,
deliver us from all evil, Our Lady,
and untie the knots that prevent us from being
united in God,
so that we, free from sin and error, may find him
in all things,
may have our hearts placed in him,
and may serve him always in our brothers and sisters.
Amen.

CHAPTER TWO

Balance

*We cannot be happy if we expect to live all the time at the
highest peak of intensity. Happiness is not a matter of intensity
but of balance and order and rhythm and harmony. Music is
pleasing not only because of the sound but because of the silence
that is in it: without the alternation of sound and silence there
would be no rhythm.*

THOMAS MERTON, *NO MAN IS AN ISLAND*

I've often had to learn lessons the hard way in life. A-brick-
falling-on-my-foot kind of hard. When my family is caught
up in the fallout from my "hard way" lessons, it's even more
painful. Hopefully, I learn these lessons even better.

When I was in my third year of law school, Philip and I
were willing to face the truth about what wasn't working for
our family. Holidays and weekends had become just another
opportunity to "get something done" rather than a time making memories with our little boy (we had only one child at the
time). Our home life was, let's say, very efficient, but it wasn't
a place of ease and renewal. Our son often got the leftovers of
our energy after we'd given so much of it to people and projects away from him. The ordinary setbacks of life often turned
into catastrophes because we didn't have the time to manage

them. Many of our problems were rooted in a lack of balance in our lives, and we recognized it. So, not long after we found out we were expecting our daughter Claire, we decided that I would turn my focus toward home after her arrival. My due date was just after graduation, so we figured I would breeze through the last months of law school, and then I would stay home full-time with our children to bring some healing and heart into our home. We determined that *later*, after the baby came, we would have time for more balance. But my baby made it clear that later was not going to work for her.

When I was four months pregnant with Claire, I came down with a cold that lingered … and lingered. When I was six months along, I was still sick. I was so determined to graduate on time that I continued to attend a full load of classes, even though my body was giving me clues that I needed to slow down. I didn't want to be a quitter; I wanted to prove to everyone that I could be a mother and still succeed academically without any favors or special treatment. I ignored how sick I was in order to achieve my goal. I figured I was being tough.

When I went to my six-month obstetric appointment, the talk was less about baby and more about my cough. I was diagnosed with pneumonia. When the doctors couldn't clear my lungs after four days at home, I was admitted to the hospital. I spent a week receiving steroids and nebulizer treatments, all the while wondering how I'd ended up in this predicament, with my life and my baby's at risk. My determination had been terribly misguided. I wasn't tough; I was foolish. Thank God I recovered and the baby was fine, but that scare forced me to examine my priorities and motivations.

I had learned my hard-way lesson.

We made major changes after I came home from the hospital. I reduced my class load at school, which meant I'd have to finish off some units after the baby was born, but it also meant we could begin living with more calm, rest, and balance right in the moment when the baby and I needed it most. That experience taught me never to ignore the warning signs that my body isn't keeping up with my plans, especially when I have a family to care for.

Philip and I are not unique in our battle with imbalance and burnout. All modern parents know how important balance is for our families; we also know how hard it is to achieve. Consider all the things we must balance as parents: work and family, work and play, work and worship, time alone with our spouse and time together with our children, time with family and time with friends, our children's schedules and our own, our need for exercise and our desire for couch time, our dreams and our budget, our children's dreams and our dreams. Most of us have to balance all those things *every day*. Whew.

Over the years since those days in law school, I've found that living a balanced life when you have children is sort of like tuning into a great song on an old radio. When we hear too much feedback, we know we're offtrack, so we turn the dial a smidge until we hear our song. We enjoy the song, but it's not long before it begins to scramble again. So again, we move the dial, searching for the song, getting the frequency just right. And there it is, but again only for a while. You see, as parents we will spend the coming years moving between activity and rest, between merriment and boredom, between ease and striving. We bring balance to our lives when we cultivate an awareness of signs that we need to shift course — to move that dial — in order to renew, to reconnect, to tune into the source of our strength and hope.

Why Balance Matters

What is the purpose of seeking balance anyway? Is it so that we can find some kind of inner nirvana in which we're detached from life's nettles and nuisances while they're happening around us? Is it so that we will be perpetually happy, calm, and unaffected by the pain or demands of the world? I don't think so. We're parents living in the world with children whose care has been entrusted to us. Our parenting mission requires us to dive into the chaos. This means our lives are filled with duty and distractions, dirt and diapers.

Yes, sometimes discipleship parenting will cost us calm and quiet, and occasionally a clean shirt. Still, we need to deal with the problem of imbalance and burnout. It's bad for the whole family — kids and parents alike. When parents feel stressed and overworked, they can't respond to their children with calmness and warmth. When kids are stressed and overscheduled, their healthy development is at risk. Without enough pauses in their days and weeks, kids not only become very moody, but they can't assimilate and integrate what they're experiencing and learning.

Life includes stress. This is inescapable. We need a little stress and resistance in our lives to learn to deal with it and grow. Even kids need an exposure to stress in order to develop a healthy stress-response system. But too much stress — stress that's either too big or too persistent — is bad for us and our children. It's the persistent stress of frazzled families that really concerns me. This is the kind of stress my family was struggling with when I was in law school. We felt like we were constantly putting out small fires — again and again, with no end in sight. Even small stressors can drag down the mental, emotional, and physical health of everyone in the family if the stress is chronic. It can happen without our noticing because we're usually engaged in what are basically wholesome, worthwhile activities. Stress can become a lifestyle choice driven by good intentions. Before we know it, the tension is palpable in our homes — we ignore or snap at one another because we're exhausted and disconnected.

In seeking a balanced life, we aren't called to climb atop some cloud on which we'll never be bothered or disturbed, but it's okay to seek retreat from the world when you or your family needs it — not to reject the world, but to engage in it with greater vitality when we walk out the door again. As disciple-parents, we can build into our homes time and space for renewal and contemplation so that we're better able to become the family God is calling us to be.

Reality Check: There's Always Enough Time

As Catholics, we recognize that time is a gift from God. We are meant to use our time to glorify him and to fulfill the mission he has in mind for us. Our calendar belongs to God. This is easy to forget, though. If we find ourselves saying frequently that we don't have enough time for the basic habits of a Christian life — worship, prayer, companionship, sharing food, offering works of mercy — then it's possible we've taken control of our time instead of offering it to God. If we take the reins of our life away from God, we'll inevitably find ourselves on a wild ride headed for a collision.

Father Wilfrid Stinissen doesn't mince words: "Most of us have a lot to do. But we can never have *too* much to do. ... When God gives us a mission, he also creates the time needed for it. If there is no time for it, then it is not a task that comes from him but, rather, a work that we have arbitrarily taken upon ourselves, a job that falls outside of his plan for our life."[1] Wow. We never have *too much* to do. A lot to do, yes. But never too much, if we've given the reins of our lives to God and we're letting him be the God of our time. If we find ourselves thinking that we don't have time to deal with a sick child or respond to a need in our community, then perhaps we've filled up our time with something that shouldn't be there. As adults, we can examine our motivations for the commitments we've made and discern in prayer where God wants us to be spending our time.

Slow Catholic Family Living

I appreciate the recent interest in "slow family living."[2] This is a small but important movement of parents making the radical choice to prioritize downtime in their homes, to choose consciously to do less away from home so they can connect more with their families. They step off the treadmill of constant activity and choose instead to savor time having fun and relaxing with their kids. Through the parents who write and speak about slow family living, I've learned how to simplify my home life so that enough breaks are built into every day and every week. When I began prioritizing these downtimes, my family realized we weren't really giving anything up. We were just making room for other things that mattered to us more.

Simplifying our lives doesn't mean we have to quit our jobs and move to a farm on a hundred acres. It just means we're being honest with ourselves about how much time our particular family needs together at home to thrive. Consider your family: Where are you now? What is and isn't working for your family? What is distracting you from building a strong family identity and resilient bond? Here are some thoughts on tackling what I consider the top three most common enemies of a balanced home: (1) extracurricular activities, (2) social engagements, and (3) technology. None of these things is bad in itself, but we need to establish clear boundaries with them, to keep them from eating up all of our family's time.

1. Extracurricular Activities

In conversations with many friends, I've noticed that over-commitment to extracurricular activities (soccer, karate, ballet, drama, swimming) has become the biggest drain in their lives, leaving everyone grumpy and disconnected. Families need lots of time to sit and be together, to fuss around the house, to play board games, to ponder big questions and small ones. When mom and dad are constantly looking at their appointment calendars, and kids are anxious about being late for their sports practices, we risk allowing our calendars to become the heart of our home and the engine that drives us.

If we find ourselves absorbed with constant activity, we

may fear on some level that unless we're always busy and frazzled, we're behind in some way. We're afraid our children will be deprived of some opportunity that other children have. We're afraid our children will fall behind in some way — developmentally, socially, or academically. We're afraid that if we step off the treadmill, even temporarily, our children won't be successful or happy. So we sign them up for sports, after-school tutoring, chess clubs, and Mandarin classes — in kindergarten! Our homes begin to revolve around the kids and their schedules. It becomes a trap. The pace of our lives creates an illusion that we're doing important things, but really it's distracting us from each other and God.

There's nothing wrong with wanting our children to be successful. It's good to have high expectations of our kids! In fact, developing follow-through and industry is an important developmental goal for kids during their school years.[3] And of course we should encourage our kids to explore their talents through classes, clubs, and similar opportunities. This is one of the ways our children might reach beyond their secure bases to explore the world, which I talked about in the last chapter. We want our kids to experience the joy and exhilaration of stretching their wings and trying new things. Still, there's no question that many families are overcommitted. It's become the norm. If you sense your family is losing too much time together because you're driving around to different sports practices, music lessons, and drama classes, perhaps it's time to turn the dial and shift your choices a bit.

You don't have to give up all extracurricular activities. Maybe your children can each choose one activity, or you can find activities that are all scheduled on only a few days a week so you are home on the other days. Think creatively. After families were becoming burned out by coordinating their kids' soccer practices and game schedules, my local homeschool group started an intergenerational soccer league in which several families got together once a week, and they all played soccer together — parents and kids of all ages. I believe that moving toward intergenerational activities is one of the best ways we can not only protect our children from burnout but also transmit our values and faith to them. I'll talk more about this in later chapters.

2. Social Engagements

Play dates and other social engagements are another time drain for many families. What seems like too much socializing for my family may not be too much for yours, but I personally become agitated if my schedule is jam-packed with social activities — especially lots of loud, frenetic group activities. I'm extremely introverted. This doesn't mean I don't like parties or social gatherings, but they tend to drain me, so I need to balance them with time at home in order to feel okay. When we have been hustling and on the go for several days in a row, my children, too, are left cranky and drained. So I try to limit our social engagements. When my children were all young, I accepted only one party invitation on the weekends, and I planned a day of recovery after a play date before we hosted or accepted an invitation to another one. Now my children are maturing. I have relaxed my rules about social engagements a little, but I try to pay attention to moods. Some weeks I have to return to my old rules so we can slow down and reconnect.

3. Technology

Many families are grappling with the new problems technology is creating in our homes: sensory processing issues, Internet safety, and virtual bullying, just to name a few. Is the solution to get rid of screens? I know a few families who don't have a television and don't permit their children to use computers for any purpose. In my home, we have only one television and our two computers remain in a central location. Our children don't have phones (with the exception of our older son, who is at college now). Frequently, though, I feel like screens are taking over my family's time and that we're having far too many conversations about them — which screen so-and-so has been hogging, or who's next to use it and for how long. I imagine having those conversations about things that really matter, like packing food for the victims of natural disasters or planting flowers! *Can I plant the next flower? I've only been planting flowers for twenty minutes! Yes, but so-and-so has been planting flowers since he woke up so it's my turn now!* So I have to make a conscious effort to keep screens in their right place in our family life — that is, on the sidelines of our existence and not at the center.[4]

How much time is appropriate for children to consume technology? Your family pediatrician will give you advice about appropriate screen limits for your children, but ultimately parents have to decide what's best. Each child is different. I try to observe my children's behavior after they use different media. Some days they can't handle anything near the maximum my pediatrician suggests; other days they seem fine.

We started a tradition several years ago that I look forward to every year. During Lent, we have a technology fast in our home on Fridays. No computers, television, gaming systems, or handheld devices are turned on the whole day, except for school purposes. My children rarely complain about our Lenten technology fasts. In fact, I think they secretly like them. Inspired by the creativity and sense of calm that flowers on those Lenten Fridays, I now call technology fasts anytime I sense my children need help breaking away from the glare of their screens.

I've never been much interested in technology. I tend to use it for purely utilitarian purposes, not for enjoyment (except for watching a movie on occasion). I had a flip phone until a few years ago when I finally got an Android phone. I appreciate my new phone, but I don't think I was missing much. Because of my skepticism about technology, I've always resisted my children getting new devices and having access to online games. I want them to enjoy books, music, art, and real toys that they can hold in their hands and love. But the rest of my family has a different opinion. Philip and all four of our children are fascinated by technology and all the latest gadgets. Even my eight-year-old is very tech savvy and can navigate my new phone better than I can! Because of my family, I do recognize the benefits of many types of media. For example, my teenage daughter, Claire, enjoys creating graphic designs with software and sharing her art online with friends. Her interest and talent helped me appreciate that some media experiences are of a better quality and more wholesome than others. Of course, I also want her to spend time creating art with her hands away from her computer. We'll continue working on getting that balance right!

Mom and Dad model for their children how to use technology responsibly and politely. We can show our kids that cell phones should be out of sight — and left unanswered — during meals and family time. They should also be turned off during Mass and during public events in which the phone ringing would distract others (movies, concerts, etc.). We can also casually share with our kids how and why we set limits and boundaries for ourselves with our devices. Through our example, our children will realize that these simple rules of etiquette really protect relationships. We can show them how to use technology to build relationships and God's kingdom, rather than walls between ourselves and others.

These three things — extracurricular activities, social engagements, and technology — routinely come up in conversations with my friends when we're complaining about being tired, stressed, and stretched. I'm sure you can add to this list. The bottom line is that our families need enough downtime to reflect and refuel. We want our children to grow up knowing what it feels like when a family chooses each other over external expectations. Through these choices, we can teach our children that time is a gift from God; we can use it wisely or foolishly just like any other gift.

How much busyness, socializing, and technology our families can handle depends on the developmental stages and unique personalities of our kids. Young families with tiny ones probably need the most simplified schedules and more home time with the phones unplugged. But even families with fidgety teenagers should ensure the family remains their children's primary source of strength and encouragement, and this requires a commitment to family connection and silencing the world regularly so we can hear ourselves and one another better.

Of course, I'm not suggesting we fold our children away in our homes like fine linens we don't want to risk soiling. Sometimes we dive into the dirt together to do some work God is calling us to do. Even when a work of mercy invites chaos, grumbling, and fatigue, even when it shakes up the calm and balance in our homes, sometimes we know God is calling us to the task. In this life of discipleship, sometimes we slow down our lives so we can catch our breath as a family, but then we're all the more prepared to offer ourselves for the benefit of somebody in need. Then, like tuning into that song on the radio, we move inward again as a family to refresh our connection, now made stronger by our willingness to serve others.

Balancing Care of Others with Self-Care

This just in: Parents have needs too! We need nourishment, work, rest, exercise, and a private prayer life. You probably know this already, but maybe you're wondering when all this is supposed to happen when you're living with children who seem to want you every moment of the day and night. We sacrifice sleep, comfort, and even personal grooming in order to meet the pressing needs of our little ones. We usually prioritize their needs because they're weaker and more vulnerable than we are physically and emotionally, so the cost of ignoring their needs is higher for them than for us. At some point, though, God wants us to practice self-care in order to renew our own vitality and strength. Sometimes loving our children means we prioritize our own needs so that we have something left to give them.

Does the thought of self-care make you a little uncomfortable? Aren't we supposed to "forget self" and serve others completely? Is it selfish or even un-Christian to consider our own needs? Certainly not.

Self-care isn't selfishness: It's actually a virtue. Let me explain. The great virtue of love includes love of God, love of neighbor, and *love of self*.[5] Jesus tells us that the two greatest commandments are: "You shall love the Lord your God with all your heart, and with all your soul, and with all your mind, and with all your strength" and "You shall love your neighbor as yourself" (Mk 12:30–31). When Christ commands us to love our neighbors as ourselves, he presumes that we love ourselves — that we love ourselves really, really well. After all, God wouldn't want us to love our neighbor by ignoring them or forgetting about them, right? So, a healthy self-love (as opposed to a sense of entitlement or superiority) is necessary for sincere love of others.

Loving ourselves includes protecting our dignity, not permitting others to use or abuse us, and finding ways to meet our own physical, emotional, and spiritual needs even when we're called to the sacred work of raising children. In Catholic virtue ethics, real virtue is the "golden mean" between two extreme character flaws. For example, humility is the golden mean between arrogance on one end and self-deprecation on the other; courage is the golden mean between recklessness on one end and cowardice on the other. Well, love is the golden mean between being a doormat and a bully, between being completely absorbed in another person and being self-absorbed, between indulging every whim of our children and neglecting their needs. *Self*-love or *self*-care is the golden mean between always putting ourselves first and always putting others first. Either extreme is unhealthy and unloving, though our culture or our personal history may tell us otherwise.

The virtue of self-care doesn't require that we spend equal time on self-care and care of others, but only that we avoid self-neglect. We offer ourselves in love to serve the needs of others, but God will always provide enough time for us to restore ourselves too. Put simply, parents have a unique responsibility to care for themselves so that they're better equipped to care for the children and others placed in their care. Parenting challenges us to handle stressful situations that can leave us strained and depleted. We need to heal from these demands so that we have the capacity to serve our families better.

Even Jesus took breaks on occasion. Scripture records him several times going off alone to pray or to rest. For example, in the Gospel of Mark, we read, "And in the morning, a great while before day, he rose and went out to a lonely place, and there he prayed" (Mk 1:35). And he insisted that his disciples do the same. Just before the familiar episode in which Jesus feeds a huge crowd with a few loaves of bread and two fishes, this exchange takes place: "The apostles returned to Jesus, and told him all that they had done and taught. And he said to them, 'Come away by yourselves to a lonely place, and rest a while.' For many were coming and going, and they had no leisure even to eat. And they went away in the boat to a lonely place by themselves" (Mk 6:30–32).

The apostles had been out ministering together in pairs, and it was a huge success. I can imagine the twelve friends were gathered around Jesus, elbowing in to give him all the details. But the crowd was growing, and the disciples hadn't eaten. One might expect Jesus to encourage them to jump right in while they have a chance to minister to these people, but he doesn't. He recognizes that his friends are tired and hungry; they need to be alone to regroup and refresh themselves before they can go on with the mission entrusted to them. Some commentaries about this passage describe the disciples as going off to a "desert place" or a "wilderness," which echoes the patterns of both Jesus and John the Baptist. The desert place is not only a space for the disciples' physical recuperation, but also for their spiritual formation.

As parents we, too, are called to serve. We, too, are Christ's disciples ministering to the hunger, sorrows, and fears of those placed in our care. We, too, need occasional desert retreats so that we can retain our fire for our mission of raising faithful children. In retreat, we remember what's most important to us; we become once again "convinced, enthusiastic, certain, and in love" with Christ.[6] This is why self-care is essential to evangelizing our children: The joy, hope, and peace that radiates from deep faith are contagious for everyone we encounter, including our kids. In the desert, we become living water from which the thirsty souls around us can drink.

Yes, sometimes being a Christian parent *does* require that we forget ourselves and our needs in order to meet the needs of others, but not always. It takes prudence and wisdom to know how to handle situations in which our children's needs conflict with our own. Here are a few questions to consider when you're facing these moments.

1. Does your child have a legitimate need that requires your immediate attention, or can it wait?
Children all have needs for nourishment, protection, comfort, affection, ritual, rest, and play (to name but a few). In the last chapter, I explained why it's so important to meet the legitimate needs of our children with tenderness and generosity. But fostering attachment doesn't necessarily require that we meet every single need *right now*. How long children can wait obviously depends on their maturity and temperament. Infants

and little babies usually have needs that require our immediate attention, and the distress they experience is real and better off avoided. But they also sleep a lot, and folks love holding and feeding babies! So if your baby is hungry, soiled, or tired, attend to her needs immediately or allow somebody else to help you. The early stage of infancy, which is so all-consuming and draining at times, passes very quickly. As kids mature, they grow increasingly capable of waiting to have their needs met.

2. Does your child have a *desire* that can wait because you have a more pressing *need*?
Desires and needs are two different kettles of fish. Sometimes a child may have a *desire* — even a very worthy one — that conflicts with our own *need* for something essential to our well-being. It's perfectly acceptable (and healthy) to prioritize your own immediate need over your child's desire. So if your child wants to go to the park, but you need a shower, your shower comes before the park. Kids may complain at first when you make the shocking choice to meet your own needs, especially if you've made a habit of ignoring your needs to say yes to their requests and wishes. Just kindly but firmly tell your child why she must wait and for how long. Don't ask your children for permission to meet your own needs ("Is it okay if I finish my sandwich first?"). Rather, explain politely that their desires will be attended to later after you've had a chance to do what you need to do for yourself ("Oh, yes, I'd love to make cookies, but first I'm going to finish my sandwich and milk").

Of course, this is meant as a guideline, not an uncompromising rule. Perhaps you'll decide to take your shower later or you'll encourage your kids to start gathering the ingredients for cookies while you finish your lunch. But I hope we parents can remind ourselves that we're not doing anyone any favors by eating crumbs off our kids' lunch plates every day and calling it a meal. We deserve to be treated with dignity too, and our children only benefit in the long run from recognizing that truth.

3. What are you doing for your children that they can do for themselves?

In our house, Philip is in charge of bringing the trash bins to the street every week for the garbage collectors, and then rolling them back to the side yard at the end of the day. I regularly grab the bins and do this job for him, just to make his life a little easier. He does the same for me. Even though we both fold and put away our own clothes after laundering them, I regularly discover that Philip has folded and placed my clothes neatly on my dresser. We offer these little acts of generosity for one another out of love; we want to lighten the burden for each other.

I've noticed, though, that too often there's a different dynamic at work in my relationship with my children. I get into a habit of doing their chores for them because I don't want to cause friction or bother them while they're playing. This habit persists, and I end up doing just about everything for them. This "helping" habit is far different from the little gifts of kindness that Philip and I offer to one another. Catholic mom and author Genevieve Kineke helped me understand the difference: "Offering to help a child with a chore can be magnanimous when he or she is discouraged or overwhelmed, but to step in regularly and finish the work will only undermine essential lessons in responsibility, time management, and accountability. Authentic love will separate acts of charity from enabling behavior, which are far from loving and are damaging to other souls."[7]

Am I really loving my children or teaching them to be self-centered? Children need our support when they are struggling with chores, but they also need to be given the opportunity to become effective, responsible, and reliable. This means they need to do their fair share of work around the house when they're old enough to handle it.

Now, I see nothing objectionable about helping my children even when they don't really need it. Loving others generously, especially within our families, includes relieving one another of burdens, even if the other person is perfectly capable of handling the burden on his or her own. I feel loved and cared for when Philip folds my clothes for me, even though I know how to do it. The fact that Philip takes those extra few minutes just because he loves me means more to me than a dozen roses! (If you're a mother who faces weekly laundry, you know I'm not kidding.)

We know we should avoid being perceived as cold and scary in our children's eyes, but we must also avoid becoming permissive and indulgent. We want to avoid both extremes. Treating our children like royalty who are too precious to be bothered with menial household tasks is unjust, because it denies them full membership in our community of love. They deserve a chance to grow into generous, self-giving members of our family. Vacuuming needs to be done; somebody needs to feed the dog; mom gets sick sometimes and can't make breakfast. Allowing our children to experience and navigate these necessary duties and occasional setbacks in a safe, loving home trains their minds and hearts to deal with the big stuff later with greater grace and maturity.

4. Can you find renewal while also meeting the needs of your child?

You may have some wonderful ideas about your desert place of renewal — where it will be and what it should look like. Perhaps you imagine praying on a bench by a duck pond, or painting at an easel with a smear of watercolor on your brow. These sanctuaries are surely part of God's plan for us, and I encourage parents to work together to ensure both mom and dad have this kind of private time for themselves. Sometimes, though, we won't be able to escape the demands of parenting when we know we need a break. This certainly happened to the first disciples. In the passage above in which Jesus brings his disciples to a deserted place to eat and rest, something unexpected happens after they arrive on the other side of the lake: "Now many saw them going, and knew them, and they ran there on foot from all the towns, and got there ahead of them. As he landed he saw a great throng, and he had compassion on them, because they were like sheep without a shepherd; and he began to teach them many things" (Mk 6:33–34).

Yep. When they get off the boat, they find people waiting there for them. So much for going off to a private retreat!

Does this sound familiar? You get up early in the morning to pray in your favorite chair by a sunny window when you hear the floor creaking down the hallway. Or you just settle down to have a cup of tea and begin turning the cover of a new book when you hear the baby stirring. Sometimes we enter our desert retreat where we unexpectedly encounter not solitude but our children, just as the disciples and Jesus encountered those followers when they got off their boat. Jesus changed his mind when he saw that crowd. He had pity on them, these souls searching for a shepherd. They had followed him into retreat the way our children follow us sometimes. There will be times when we can attend to our children and return to our delicious break, but at other times it won't work out.

We still have options. If we think creatively, we can find "little deserts" — retreats for our souls — right in our own living rooms surrounded by our children. You can be a disciple leading your children into retreat with you just as Jesus and his disciples did with that crowd. When you find yourself in such a situation, search for ways to meet your own needs while ministering to your children. What are your most pressing needs right now? How do you most find comfort and refreshment? Consider your child's personality and interests. How might you find a little rest and peace while nurturing your child? Sometimes just getting outside can change our outlook and ability to cope with parenting's little stressors. Go for a long walk with your little ones in a stroller, or take a bike ride with the kids and have a picnic at a park. Lie on the grass and stare up at the sky, send your kids on a nature treasure hunt while you drink iced tea, or keep a family cloud journal. Do whatever makes you feel both connected and refreshed.

My home has a lot of windows and three sliders facing out into our backyard garden. When I know the kids need to get outside and I need to unwind a little, I tell them that I'm going to sit in my chair out in the back garden to read. Then, I sit. Without fail, one by one they all come out to see what I'm doing and end up digging in the garden or reading beside me. If you find respite in a good book like I do, try instituting a family reading hour (or half hour). If you're all cozied up together with your books, even little ones will be willing to calm down for a few minutes.

Then there's the issue of sleep. If you have a young baby, you may struggle with sleep deprivation. When we're new parents, well-meaning folks tell us to "sleep when the baby sleeps," which is great advice, but when you have more than one child this seems impossible. Often older children no longer nap, or they are engaged in activities away from home. When we had babies in our home, I instituted an afternoon "quiet hour": Everyone was required to stay in bed for an hour; they could either read or listen to music quietly. I sometimes permitted (non-beeping) toys with the understanding that play was to be quiet and in bed. Everyone benefited from family quiet hour. My preschoolers inevitably fell asleep; they were tired too. My older children had some quiet time alone to think, to make up stories in their heads, or just stare at the patterns on their blanket. Solitude is essential to the flourishing of the human imagination, so even if they don't seem to like it at first, insist that older children participate in your family quiet time. Reassure them that they aren't being punished, but rather that you believe the whole family could use some mental and physical rest. I used our family quiet time to nap at first, but eventually when I no longer needed those naps, I continued the quiet times so that I could have an hour of silence to refuel. An entire chapter on play is coming up, but let me mention here that, just like our kids, we need time for laughter, creativity, and release, because without them we become emotionally and intellectually stagnant. We actually experience *entropy*. Dr. Stuart Brown explains: "Many studies have demonstrated that people who continue to play games, who continue to explore and learn throughout life, are not only much less prone to dementia and other neurological problems, but are also less likely to get heart disease and other afflictions that seem like they have nothing to do with the brain. ... When we stop playing, we stop developing, and when that happens, the laws of entropy take over — things fall apart."[8]

When we stop playing, we stop developing; when we stop developing, things fall apart. Just because we're parents doesn't mean we have to skip our need for creative living. Meet your own need for play right alongside your child. Are you a tinkerer, an artist, a card player, a baker? When you're feeling drained, shift gears. I've found an escape lately at the sewing table. Just fifteen minutes of cutting, piecing, and trimming, and I seem to perk up. It really works. So set aside your to-do list and get out the watercolors, find an old radio to take apart, or don that chef's hat. Share your passion with your children! You'll find some creative release while building memories with your children.

In practicing self-care, you're setting an important example for your kids. Some people can't slow down because they need to feel useful. They equate their personal value with productivity, earning, and competing. When you prioritize your own well-being, you are teaching your kids to value their passions and the importance of exploring them, even if they produce nothing more than memories and good cheer.

Balancing Work and Family

Though I became a full-time mom after law school, I tried

to find ways to work on some legal projects. For the first few years, I worked about eight hours a week in a criminal defense law firm. It was fascinating. However, when even this arrangement proved too disruptive to our family life, I transitioned to a home-based brief and motion writing practice. After the birth of my third child, I gave up practicing law altogether, though I still maintain my license for practical reasons (and my son Aidan frequently poses intriguing legal questions which result in my law books getting a bit of dusting off).

My focus during those early years was on bringing a sense of rhythm and rapport to our family and on creating a real home, not just a place we came to sleep at the end of the day. I believe that this single decision Philip and I made saved our family. We can never get back those years in law school when we all suffered to some extent, but we learned a hard-way lesson about what really matters to us. I have never regretted that choice.

Given my own struggles with balancing paid work and the needs of my family, it surprises many people to learn that I don't think all mothers need to forgo full-time paid work. Women bring a unique perspective to discussions in the parish, the boardroom, and the public square. When that perspective is absent, society suffers. Saint John Paul the Great said it well:

> Without the contribution of women, society is less alive, culture impoverished, and peace less stable. Situations in which women are prevented from developing their full potential and from offering the wealth of their gifts should therefore be found profoundly unjust, not only to women themselves but to society as a whole. ... It is necessary to strive convincingly to ensure that the widest possible space is open to women in all areas of culture, economics, politics, and ecclesial life itself, so that all human society is increas-

ingly enriched by the gifts proper to masculinity and femininity.[9]

On the other hand, when moms are absent from home, their children may suffer. This is simply a reality we can't ignore. The nature of some jobs makes it difficult to provide the kind of attunement and guidance children need. It goes without saying that neither parent should put his or her own career goals ahead of the well-being of their children. But mothers have a special role to play in protecting the heart of the home and nurturing children, especially very small children. Working full-time makes fulfilling and enjoying that role more challenging, but not impossible.

As they pray for discernment about whether mom will work away from home, how much she'll work, and when she should make that transition, parents should enter into a period of discernment. In discerning the path for your family, pray that you will be open to God's will, whatever it is, and that he'll reveal it clearly to you. Ask him to free you from any attachments to honor, wealth, or admiration, and to remove any shadows of self-doubt. Seek advice from a spiritual director and read books comparing your options. Consider honestly how children thrive and how your particular family will best thrive. Make a list comparing the pros and cons of both choices. Ask God to give you a sense of peace and confidence about the right option. Whatever decision you make, it need not be final; you can change your mind.

If you decide to return to work, investigate your childcare options and learn what to look for in quality childcare. Infants and toddlers might experience unhealthy levels of the stress hormone cortisol in large daycares.[10] When they're in nonparent childcare, stress levels are lower in children when they're matched with one warm, attuned, and consistent caregiver rather than a team of caregivers who change frequently. So if you have a child younger than three, if possible, find a loving family member who can provide care for you, or perhaps a caregiver who can come into your home to care for only your child. Have your child and the caregiver spend time together before you begin work, so your child feels safe with the new caregiver. Stress levels are also lower in children who spend fewer hours per day in nonparent childcare. So perhaps both spouses can arrange their working hours to reduce the number of hours their child is in daycare.

If you choose to work outside your home for pay, then you will bring your natural gifts to the workplace, in addition to the skills you've gained as a parent. If you're a mother, and you choose to focus on mothering and homemaking, remember that this is work too, even if our society overlooks its value. All moms work! For me, I knew through prayer and a long period of discernment that God was calling me home full-time. Many people disapproved. *You're just about to take off. You've been preparing for this moment for years; why walk away? You have a responsibility to use your talent and education.* I stepped out in faith, even if it made sense only to Philip and me. My cooperation alone was a grace, rooted in the confidence and courage that God breathed into me.

I learned that when I show up for God, in his delight he will surprise me with little gifts. He has showered me with graces I never saw coming. I came home for my children and husband, but I have benefited as much, if not more, than they. Aside from the things I've done that directly benefit my family, I have grown personally as a woman. I've had time to deepen my prayer life and read more for pleasure; I've learned how to sew and knit, and even how to ferment vegetables; I'm now a bread baker, writing teacher, podcaster, and blogger; I've cultivated a life of beauty, leisure, and contemplation. I share this not to sell you on making the choice I made, but to encourage you to seek God's will, and then to trust it. Don't be afraid. His generosity will blow you away!

Our lives will always be filled with things that need to be

done and opportunities for filling up our calendars. When we're stressed out about overcommitments, the workload of parenting, or finding balance between paid work and family life, we're usually dealing with some kind of fear: fear of what others think of us or our kids; fear of what will happen if we don't finish this thing here and perform that thing there. God doesn't intend for us to live this way. God wants us to lean on him, to trust him to help us get the job done, whatever it is. We learn more about ourselves, our deepest purpose, our greatest gifts, and our hidden talents, when we follow God's lead in how we spend our time. When we offer our calendars to God, he will show us the way to living a balanced family life and to greater clarity about what's really important to us. With God's help, we'll make small decisions each day that will have a giant impact on the long-term happiness of our whole family.

CHAPTER THREE
Play

*The true object of all human life is play. Earth is a task garden;
heaven is a playground.*

G. K. CHESTERTON

When my son Dominic was seven years old, I taught his catechism class every Wednesday afternoon at our parish. One Wednesday, after we parked alongside the parish building, I was pulling my canvas book bag from our van while Dominic swung on the seat and the back interior ledge of the van. He popped out of the van and skipped over the cement squares on the sidewalk leading up to the door of the Faith Formation building. Then he planted both feet firmly on the ground, gripped the handle of the door, and leaned gradually back to discover how much of his weight it would take before the door opened. After we collected my teacher's box from the office, he ran the entire way to our classroom, singing about something I can't recall. I couldn't help smiling as I witnessed him encounter with each step some new piece of the world. I saw my boy on a blissful, full-body adventure with his eyes, legs, arms, mind, and voice completely engaged. He seemed so free.

Dominic wasn't swinging, leaning, running, and singing

for any specific purpose. He couldn't help himself, really. I think Dominic experienced that day something that God intends for all of us. Play is part of the way we humans explore and express our passion and joy. It drives our innermost creativity — not just in children, but in all people. Yet, we can overlook its importance. We assume it's unimportant, even a waste of time, because it doesn't produce anything we can sell or measure for the most part (unless we're a toy inventor or play scientist, I guess). Because we tend to measure "happiness" by competitive success, not interior fulfillment, we often don't have much use for play. It sometimes seems that the Western formula for life is work a lot, makes oodles of cash, and rest only as much as is necessary to avoid a heart attack. Sometimes we tolerate our kids playing just because it keeps them occupied. We really should do more than tolerate it: We should celebrate it and recognize it for what it is, especially when it comes to our families.

Why Kids Need Play

When grown-ups "play," we often think of it as time off from our usual work responsibilities. For us, play is about relaxation and leisure and refueling ourselves mentally and physically so that we can return to our work refreshed. But this isn't true for kids. For them, play *is* their work. I hate to describe it as "work," because I don't think play has to be productive or practical to be worthwhile, but the fact is kids need to play in order to develop normally. When kids play, they're learning about the world: how things feel, smell, dissolve, crumble, slip, and resist. They're gathering valuable information about how things work in time and space, through cause and effect.

At every stage of development, children are pressing on to new phases of maturity through their play. For example, when toddlers are playing, they're often practicing their language skills. To us, they seem merely to be jabbering away, but they're really building their vocabularies. When Dominic was leaping, running, and bouncing that Wednesday, he was strengthening his gross motor skills and even improving his neuromuscular development. Play helps to shape a child's brain so that he can be truly creative and innovative.[1] In fact, play is so critical to a child's healthy development that the United Nations has recognized it as a basic human right of every child.[2]

Children need play because it's often how they make sense of their struggles and worries. They recreate them within their play. A child who needs a boost of confidence after a setback at school might choose to play at something he's really good at, like building forts or drawing. A child who is struggling with a fear or a frustration might try to work it out through fantasy play. He imagines himself a king in his castle made of pillows, defending his stuffed animals against intruders, and after many close calls, he conquers all the bad guys. This kind of play helps children move toward interior rest.

Notice I've been describing unstructured play. In the last chapter, I explained how difficult it is for many families to live a healthy, balanced lifestyle in our society which places such emphasis on providing opportunities for children to engage in extracurricular "enrichment" activities. Another problem created by this pressure is that kids have far less time for unstructured play.[3] Kids need to experience unstructured play in order to move through normal stages of "play development."[4]

Babies and toddlers engage in play to experience and understand objects — what they feel, taste, or smell like. The older toddler plays imaginatively, pretending his toys are different objects (he puts his bear on his head and says "hat"), or he might pretend to be other people (he growls on all fours and announces that he's a bear). When hours of mommy-and-me classes press in on a little child's time for gumming and twisting his toys, something is certainly lost.

In the preschool years, kids begin to explore social roles in fantasy play. They pretend they're a mommy, a chef, or a nun.

These little ones are on high alert and watch the grown-ups around them with a keen eye. They practice and experiment with what they see. If your child sees you picking tomatoes in the garden, she will imitate this action in her play — pretending a block is a tomato and plopping it in a little basket — just for the sake of doing what she's observed you doing. Young children also use play to deal with anxiety and to express their wishes and fears.

Around the age of eight, children transition to fully co-operative play in which they make up games together, full of rules and shared expectations. An old-fashioned game of freeze tag transforms into backward tag or one involving a rock held by an unidentified player. A game of marbles over several days becomes a marble club, with the members organizing their leadership and making plans to erect a Marble Club Hut in one member's backyard.

When my oldest child, Aidan, was about eight years old, he and several other friends created what I can only describe as a complex alternate reality when we attended our weekly homeschool park days. It was fantasy play, but very sophisticated. The whole game started when a group of girls dumped a bucket of water on the boys. Two opposing teams emerged from this insult: the Anti-Bucket Squad and the Fairy Clan. This was a pretty amiable battle, involving mostly dumping water on each other or sparring with foam batons. They would take prisoners from one another's groups and negotiate exchanges. No child was ever injured, but reflecting back, I guess it's possible feelings were hurt on occasion. They seemed to work out their differences without grown-up interference. Each group ended up creating ranks for their armies and incorporating rules about what a soldier needed to do to for promotion in rank. When they weren't fighting one another in battles, each group practiced their warfare skills and made strategic plans for how to conquer the other team. This game evolved over five or six *years*.

It's through generating this kind of game-play that these older children learn something about give-and-take, compromise, fairness, and friendship. They come to understand the needs and feelings of others on a level that calls them to accountability, honesty, and generosity. They gain awareness about how their expectations are more or less reasonable, how their choices make others feel, and how to plan and implement an idea.

Yet, if these children go directly from school to karate, then to a piano lesson, then home for dinner, then out again for their Girl Scout meeting, they won't have the unstructured time necessary for this kind of creative play with friends. Before parents started feeling pressured to fill up every minute of their children's lives with something physically challenging or intellectually enriching, children had more time to be children. When I was a kid, I remember doing chores after school, then hanging out in my front yard, kicking a ball around, poking in the dirt, or cooking up stories and dramas full of danger, mystery, or intrigue.

Kids also used to have more time just to think, alone. Lord Byron said, "In solitude is where we are least alone." Alone? You mean, no phone or iPad? Won't everyone think I'm sick? Young adults (and some older ones …) are so accustomed to constant connection with others that even when they're in a room by themselves without other physical bodies around, they rarely have an opportunity to let their minds settle. For the sake of our children, perhaps we can remind ourselves that just because we are accustomed to something doesn't mean it's good for us.

Give him that solitary time for play when his curiosity and ideas can really simmer, and your child's natural creative genius will emerge effortlessly. No tutors. No programs. No gimmicks. Just one child and the imagination God gave him: that's enough to change the world. Indeed, after finishing his morning lessons in Latin, French, and reading, as a young boy C. S. Lewis would squirrel himself away in the "Little End Room" in his childhood home. There he created in writing a place called "Animal Land," inhabited by mythologized, dressed animals.[5] Surely his early well-nurtured and deeply developed imagination eventually led Lewis to create his magnificent *Chronicles of Narnia*. I wonder what would have become of Narnia if little Clive Staples Lewis had never had that time alone to think, if he had been dragged out to soccer practices because it was good for his future.

As emphasized in the last chapter, I am not dismissing organized activities and clubs. There I argued that kids need a recognizable balance in their lives between busyness and quiet, between social activity and solitude. They also need a balance between organized activity, in which Big People guide them by reason of their superior wisdom, and free play, in which they can lose themselves in what they are doing without our interference. This kind of quiet thinking time helps our children know themselves better.[6] As I will discuss below, it may also bring them into encounter with the divine.

How to Play with Your Kids: Tips for Serious Parents

Shared play is a universal phenomenon across all human cultures. In fact, no society ever survived without it.[7] Large social groups need play to thrive, and so do microcosms of community like the family. Playing with our children is one of the best ways we can foster closeness with them, so that we can move from a superficial connection to a deeper, more meaningful one.[8]

The connection and communion created by playing together reflects the Trinitarian dimension of human relationships within the family. The give-and-take, compromise, exchange, and intimacy of people laughing and having fun together reflect the creative love and collaboration of the Trinity. Play allows us to meet one another without too much risk, yet with real vulnerability and mirth. We're practicing together the virtues of courage and fairness, and what it feels like to experience loss and surrender. These are just a few aspects of play that can bring greater vibrancy to our homes.

Find Those Floaty Moments

There are different types of family play. Families can have moments of spontaneous playfulness, when they're just joking around or sharing something funny or enjoyable, whatever that means to that family. These moments float over us — easy, unexpected. If we're too distracted or uptight, we'll miss out on those moments of easy exuberance and joy.

I once taught the virtue of *eutrapelia* to my Catholic girls group. I had newly discovered this virtue. Though it sounds like a skin disorder, it is actually the virtue of being playful! It's been mostly neglected by moral theologians (which is odd, because most moral theologians I've met really know how to have fun), but Saint Thomas Aquinas championed eutrapelia. For him, play is necessary for the body to recover after a lot of physical labor, but, even more importantly, it's necessary for the soul which requires rest from the even harder work of prayer.[9] While certain forms of play are certainly sinful (obscene or crass play, or spending excessively on entertainment while neglecting the needs of the poor), Aquinas thought that a lack of play or playfulness can also be sinful. The golden mean between too much and too little play is eutrapelia: having a lightness of being, a playful attitude, and enjoying mirth at appropriate times.

So perhaps we can consider this: As parents, how can we approach family life with a lighter, more playful attitude? This isn't about being a comedian; it's about being lighthearted. When you can joke around and engage with your children in fun banter, recognize the absurdity in everyday situations, or chuckle at the inevitable silly gaffes we humans make, being together as a family is a lot more fun. When you let your guard down and giggle with your preschooler after singing a funny song, or get into a harmless poking match with your teenager as he's headed off to a friend's house, believe it or not, you're building a distinct way for your whole family to know and trust one another. These fun exchanges create a light, open emotional atmosphere in your home. Laughing together as a family can make scary things seem less scary and overwhelming circumstances appear more manageable. And although it might seem counterintuitive, it dissolves anger like magic.

These spontaneous moments may even be more important than organized play times, because they set the basic tone for how we interact with one another. Catholic psychologist and radio host Dr. Gregory Popcak often says that "rules without rapport equals rebellion." He's absolutely right. If our kids get the impression that our time together as a family is mostly about duty, schedules, responsibility, and rules, in the long run, they won't be committed to our ideals or expectations. A playful relationship with our kids builds rapport and connection so that the rules and responsibilities in our home flow naturally from that kinship, rather than something that feels imposed on them from the top down.

Some of the seven building blocks are easier for me to live out than others. Because I tend to avoid conflict, I struggled for several years with setting firm boundaries with my kids. I didn't want to disappoint them, so I had a hard time saying no or sticking to my no when I said it. So, merciful discipline — which is nonpunitive, yet firm and consistent — is a building block that I must work on diligently and intentionally. On the other hand, play is one of the easy building blocks for me. I grew up in difficult circumstances, but there was plenty of laughter, and for this I'm grateful. I have a naturally playful spirit with my kids. We have inside jokes and laugh together easily. I arm wrestle with them, moonwalk for them down our hallway, and do kind of dumb things like my "Mommy rockets": I let one of my kids sit on my feet while I'm on the ground in front of our couch, then I launch them forward into the air to land on the couch (I have it under control and so far nobody has been injured, but I'm not necessarily recommending you do this). They're all getting too big for Mommy rockets, so maybe they'll have to start launching me instead, but I can still beat all of them in arm wrestling.

I've found this playfulness to be especially helpful when raising teenagers, who often struggle with self-doubt and emotional flooding. I seem to connect with my teenagers quickly because of my sense of humor. I think it helps them not to take themselves so seriously, and it definitely makes me seem approachable to them, so the lines of communication and trust remain open. And perhaps most importantly, having a playful outlook on my role as a mom really helps me keep things in perspective and allows me to tap into the joy that God wants me to experience in my vocation. (You will notice there is no "Clean Laundry Room" building block. I'm hoping it isn't necessary for raising joyful disciples, because if it was, I'd be in trouble!)

Plan Family Play Time

Most families nowadays are apart for much of the day, so how can we ensure we have enough play time together? We need a preplanned or organized time for shared games, amusement, and exploration. Many families I know set aside one time slot a week for family fun. Everyone in their home knows that on *that* night (or morning or afternoon), there will be no sports practices, teen gatherings, business dinners, or laundry loads that can top the importance of mom, dad, and children all joining together to share some play and leisure time. It doesn't really matter what you do; what matters is that it becomes a family ritual and a way of building a history together. Here are some ideas that work well in my family:

Like many families, the Cameron-Smiths especially love **family movie nights**. Many movies appeal to kids and parents alike. My whole family shares an affection for *The Love*

Bug, Benji, Cars, and *October Sky*.[10] We also enjoy watching old movies together. A few of our favorites: *Bringing Up Baby* (1938) starring Katharine Hepburn and Cary Grant, and *How Green Was My Valley* (1941) starring Roddy McDowell and Maureen O'Hara. Kids can enjoy great, classic films, but you have to pick titles that appeal to them, and you have to be aware of potential problem content. In his book *The Best Old Movies for Families,* film critic Ty Burr offers advice for selecting age-appropriate classic films in different genres.

Family game night is another favorite in my home. We definitely love board games, but when you walk down a game aisle in a toy store, the possibilities seem endless. Why not start by sharing some of your favorite childhood board games with your kids? Of course, you're not limited to board games on game night: You can play card games, yard games, or made-up games. Cards are cheap and easy to store, and they're a great way to build those fine motor skills in your little ones. If you have small kids, you can teach them War and Go Fish, then branch off from there to Crazy Eights, Snap, and Five in a Row. Kids over ten can learn to play poker. (Watch out. They're sneaky!)[11]

Do you have a sore loser in your home? Children under five frequently become distressed when they lose a game. Older siblings become annoyed because this younger child cries or has a tantrum anytime he loses. There may be a biological explanation for this behavior. Young children have underdeveloped areas of the brain, which make it difficult for them to handle loss and frustration, even if in reality it's as insignificant as losing a board game.[12] If you have a preschooler who has this problem, try cooperative games in which the purpose is to work together toward some goal rather than playing to defeat one another.[13] Eventually, kids outgrow this stage and can handle defeat with more equanimity. For a few children, this can take a while. I'm not suggesting we shield our kids from disappointment forever. Facing the reality that they can't always be the best, the greatest, the winner is a natural and healthy part of growing up.[14] But when they're younger than five, they probably can't understand this, so I do think it's okay to emphasize cooperative games during family game night. Maybe our family fun ideas don't appeal to you. What does your family delight in? What do you talk about? If you have a family of musicians, form a family band or small chamber orchestra, or stage a singing contest or talent show. If you all love acting and the dramatic arts, spend an evening putting on skits, playing charades, or attending the theater. If you all love food, you can prepare and enjoy an elaborate meal or plan a family cookbook together. Sports lovers can plan an afternoon of flag football. Kids all studying the same foreign language? During your family play time, you can declare that only that particular language may be spoken in your home. Make it even more fun by preparing and sharing cuisine from that country. Talk it over as a family and come up with a list of things you'd like to do together during your family play time.

What if your family has a wide age range of children or drastically different interests? We have this issue in our home. My oldest child is eleven years older than my youngest. Of course, we should make some effort to find activities that we can all enjoy together. But perhaps on occasion one parent can do one thing with the little ones while the other parent does something else with the big kids; then later everyone can gather together for some hot cocoa and cookies. In our home, our girls love crafting and the boys love gaming, so sometimes our family night will involve gluing fabric butterflies in one room and playing some mega-super-deluxe computer game in the next room. This works for us!

Child-Led Play: Say Yes (at Least Sometimes)
Now let's talk about child-led play — those times when your kids ask you to join them in their own play world, whether it's pretending to be pirates, having a tea party, or playing with

a dollhouse. Sometimes we parents are flummoxed at these invitations. Heck, we're downright uncomfortable. "Um, sure, honey, in a while, after I finish disinfecting this diaper pail here (*this job will never end … thank God*)." Some parents are comfortable playing board games, but they don't feel comfortable playing horsies with their preschoolers. Why is this? Adults tend to like play that involves clearly defined rules and outcomes, but we're less comfortable with open-ended fantasy play. We're not sure what to do with this kind of play. *What are the rules? What's the goal?* Open-ended play is tremendously beneficial to children, and they're usually pretty good at it, so take the plunge and let your child lead you!

At particularly sensitive, emotional times kids may prefer to connect with us on their terms, in their way, and this is often through play. Now let's be realistic: It's perfectly fine to say no to some of your child's invitations to play. However, if you sense the invitation is your child's way of asking for help or connecting with you, then say yes if at all possible. While playing with your daughter and her dollhouse, she may gaze at the figures and begin talking about a friend hurting her feelings at school by leaving her out of a game. If nothing comes up in conversation, no biggie. She may not use this particular opportunity to open up, but spending this time with you is still her way of checking in with her safe harbor. (Pssst, that's you!)

In other places in this book, I underscore how important it is for parents to take the lead in providing and caring for their children. Children shouldn't move into the caretaker role. This can be a delicate dance on some days, but we have to inspire dependence in our children; we have to be the answer to their attachment hungers. So I don't usually allow my children to "parent" me. This means I certainly don't allow them to boss me around or move boundaries; it also means I never leave them feeling like I can't handle mothering them or providing what they need. However, in play, we can allow a child to be the parent and we can be the child. This is a great way for children to practice their caretaking instincts, and it makes for plenty of giggles when Mommy needs a nap and sucks her thumb. However, at the end of the play, we make clear to our child that we're returning now to the real world; we're the mommy or daddy again and we will feed, protect, and care for her.

Everyday Ritual as Play

Finally, don't overlook ritual and tradition as a way to play with your kids. When we turn ordinary moments into little opportunities for connection or celebration, we infuse our lives with a sense of playful wonder. We can create a warm, welcoming home environment not only through big celebrations or observances on holidays and holy days, but also through the everyday patterns of life — patterns that our children recognize and find comforting. Family therapist Kym John Payne writes: "Meaning hides in repetition: We do this every day or every week because it matters. We are connected by the things we do together. In the tapestry of childhood what stands out is not the splashy, blow-out trip to Disneyland but the common threads that run throughout and repeat: the family dinners, the nature walks, reading together at bedtime (with a hot water bottle at our feet on winter evenings), Saturday morning pancakes."[15]

Do you have daily and weekly rituals like the ones Payne is talking about? "Common threads" that help your kids feel secure and comforted? In my family, these little rituals seem to anchor our days and weeks. They also provide easy opportunities for play. I think I enjoy them as much as my children do. When my youngest, Lydia, was a toddler and still nursing, we tended to wake at the same time in the morning. We adopted a little wake-up "celebration": Lydia would extend her little hand to me palm up, and I would sing and perform the fingerplay song "Round and Round the Garden" on her palm. Then she would extend the other hand so I could repeat the fingerplay song on that palm, followed by a round of "This Little Piggy Went to the Market" on the toes of both chubby feet. I've always had special rituals with my children when my husband travels. We eat out for one meal, and I let them sleep on the futon in our office on the night he's returning from his trip. There are many more of these playful rituals. They give my children a sense of comfort and quiet expectation.

Play and Discipleship

So far we've explored the developmental and emotional benefits of play for children, and the power of playfulness to build rapport between ourselves and our kids. Play also has an important spiritual dimension that we don't want to miss. By giving a child not only the gift of childhood playtime, but a childlike playful spirit that he carries with him into adulthood, we'll help him on his path to discipleship with Christ. Does this seem a stretch? Hear me out.

First, our inclination to play is not only put there by God, but it reflects God in us.[16] God must be a great player! Just imagine how much fun he had creating the world. He's all-powerful; he could have created the world in a snap — a world that was functional, useful, and got the job done. But he took his time, painting the world with shadows and light, with color and texture, dabbing here, speckling there. What a blast! The imprint of God's play is all around us, reminding us of his creativity and delight in his creation. And that imprint is on us, too, when *we* play. By encouraging a child's play and his growing playful nature, that image of God in him becomes ever more illumined.

Second, when we surrender to play, we're participating not only in a childlike activity on earth; we're anticipating our freedom in heaven. Whether we're lost in a book, rebuilding an engine, sewing a dress, or drawing a horse, we forget ourselves. We let down our guard for a while; we even suspend judgment and ambition. We become absorbed in some other world, attuned to the creative potential within ourselves. As theologian of play Jurgen Moltmann sees it, when we play, we "anticipate our liberation and with laughing rid ourselves of the bonds which alienate us from real life."[17] In our play, during those moments of creative self-forgetting, we experience a little of that freedom from pain, disease, and alienation which will be our reward in heaven. If we only encourage our children to work hard, and dismiss play as frivolous, they will never enjoy this Great Anticipation.

Third, play opens a door to friendship with God. In his autobiography, *Surprised by Joy*, C. S. Lewis talks about the role of his childhood play on his eventual conversion to Christianity. For him, joy was absolutely essential to his experience of the transcendent God, and his play was the first place he experienced a transcendent kind of joy. He thought it isn't an accident that play is fun. We find joy in play precisely because God's own joyful nature is moving toward us. Lewis sees in play an effortless avenue to joy, and joy in turn casts upon us that "bright shadow" of holiness.[18] He recalls an experience when this bright shadow drifted into his play:

> The first is itself the memory of a memory. As I stood beside a flowering currant bush on a summer day there suddenly arose in me without warning, and as if from a depth not of years but of centuries, the memory of that earlier morning at the Old House when my brother had brought his toy garden to the nursery. It is difficult to find words strong enough for the sensation which came over me; Milton's "enormous bliss" of Eden (giving the full, ancient meaning to "enormous") comes somewhere near it.[19]

Lewis, but a little a child, stood before that flowering bush quietly contemplating, and something significant happened in his young heart and mind. There was something stirring in him:

an unnamed desire. That desire eventually led to his conversion from atheism to Christianity. The joy Lewis experienced was different from the happiness a child feels on Christmas morning or the sensorial delight of eating chocolate. The joy of play for him placed in his heart a longing — a longing only satisfied by an encounter with the divine.

Play wasn't the end for Lewis, but it was certainly a means to an end: communion with God.[20] He believed those little moments of joy he experienced in play were precursors to the fuller joy of his relationship with Christ. Play-joy opens us up to holy-joy. I'm sure it's no coincidence that those moments in my life when I've experienced the deepest spiritual connection to God are often preceded by periods during which I've opened my heart and my schedule to lots of laughter, mirth, creating, and playing.

I think Lewis was on to something even more exciting. He was already encountering Christ in his play when he was a child. Christ was breaking into his world, playing with him. Can you imagine any friendship that doesn't involve some kind of shared play, pleasure, and laughter? Our friendship with God is no different. God plays with us, I'm sure of it. I think he loves to play hide-and-seek with me. I often stumble upon little treasures ("spiritual toys") that he leaves for me to find. The small graces that we experience every day reflect God's playful nature and his desire to deepen his friendship with us. The joy of play is not only a precursor to heaven; it is heaven entering into our world.

So, we celebrate and encourage a child's play, not only because he needs it for his physical and emotional development and for his secure connection to us, but because he needs it on his path toward real discipleship. He needs to play in order to experience that bright shadow of heavenly joy where Christ sits down and plays with him. As disciple-parents, we need to play, too. And that is why we are so blessed to have children, the play experts! Children really know how to play, but we have mostly forgotten. Christ told people to observe and become like little children; I don't think he meant it as a metaphor. Through playing with our children and contemplating them in play, we might begin to possess a more playful attitude toward all of life. Then, we'll begin to understand and thirst for heavenly play, and our own spirituality and friendship with Christ will bloom.

CHAPTER FOUR

Merciful Discipline

He will feed his flock like a shepherd,
he will gather the lambs in his arms,
he will carry them in his bosom,
and gently lead those that are with the young.
ISAIAH 40:11

We Catholics have defined ourselves distinctively by our moral
lives. That distinctiveness is found in the virtue of mercy.
FATHER JAMES KEENAN, SJ, *THE WORKS OF MERCY*

Ah, discipline. The topic that sells more parenting books than any other. At this point in our time together, let me plant a stake firmly in this proposition: Catholic parents need a paradigm shift, not another method for fixing children who aren't broken. Dr. Deborah MacNamara gets it right: "The focus of discipline has become myopically focused on providing the right consequences to shape behavior into a mature form. These methods miss the big developmental picture — discipline is what we do while waiting for maturity to unfold."[1] Our children don't need to be fixed; they just need to grow up. Maturity is the only real answer to behavior problems.

The Purpose of Catholic Discipline

Mercy is at the heart of our Catholic faith; it defines us as a people. What is mercy? My moral theology professor, Father James Keenan, used to say, "Mercy is the willingness to enter into the chaos of another."[2] He meant that when we respond in mercy to people in need — even when it's messy, loud, and ugly — we're reflecting God's mercy as he works to heal the wounded and bring order to chaos.

If mercy is the willingness to enter into the chaos of another, then parents have many opportunities to practice mercy with their children. We understand chaos! As merciful Catholic parents, discipline is about bringing order to the chaos of immaturity. Practicing merciful discipline doesn't mean we let our kids "off the hook." Not at all. It means we're willing to enter the chaos of a child's mind to understand the need or emotion behind a behavior, especially one that is causing him or others to suffer. From that place of mercy, we grasp the fuller picture of what that child needs to move toward maturity.

Disciplining for the Long Term

Sometimes even those of us drawn to more empathic approaches to parenting sense that we've taken a wrong turn in the way we handle discipline. It's very likely that, for most of us, a combination of our old wounds and a lack of insight can create a perfect storm when we encounter problems with our children. As I explained in chapter 1 on love, our old wounds can haunt us, causing us to react rather than respond to our children. Either an attachment issue or some other experience can keep us locked into unhelpful relationship patterns. We don't make any kind of conscious choice in how we handle a problem — we just react.

Many parents also fall into the trap of trying to find the perfect discipline method. They rely on a series of superficial fixes for problem behavior, but these never work for very long. They think they haven't found the right method yet, but really they're looking at short-term fixes to what is actually a maturity problem, and maturity is a long-term process. They see an annoying or inappropriate behavior and they want to stop it now. Completely understandable. We do want to stop problem behavior. Unfortunately, when we limit ourselves to short-term fixes, which are really efforts to control our children, over time we find ourselves resorting to harsher forms of discipline out of desperation. We yell and nag so much that our kids avoid making eye contact with us when we walk in the room; our time together as a family degenerates quickly into a power struggle between ourselves and our kids. Bribes, yelling, threatening, and spanking might work to stop the behavior in the moment, but in the long run these choices damage the connection and trust between ourselves and our kids without teaching our kids anything but that they want to avoid "the mean mommy voice."

Merciful discipline isn't about punishment or even behavior management. Did you know the word *discipline* is derived from the Latin word *discipulus*, which means pupil? Indeed, the word *disciple* is derived from the same Latin noun. Through our discipline, we teach and guide our children as Jesus taught and guided his disciples. What do we want our children to learn through our discipline? We want them to gain wisdom, moral sensitivity, and good judgment. We hope our child's heart is transformed so that eventually his well-formed conscience guides him when we're not there. We want our children to do the right thing not because they're afraid of us, but because they've internalized Christian values and morals. As they mature, we help our children envision who they want to become, and then we help them understand how their acts and choices shape who they're becoming. Ultimately, we want our kids to do the right thing, at the right time, for the right reasons.

Merciful discipline helps children become psychologically integrated as they develop self-regulation and emotional balance through the cultivation of moral virtue. This is a long-term approach to discipline. Viewed this way, we can see that our children's misbehavior provides us with an opportunity to guide them on their path of discipleship. We can educate them in how to understand and manage their emotions and how to recognize and respect the feelings and perspectives of others. This is far less likely to happen if we use harsh, punitive discipline. As Dr. Douglas Davies explains:

> When a parent is shouting, calling a child names, or threatening to abandon her, the child pays more attention to the parent's intense emotions (and to her own fearful arousal) than to the moral value the parent is asserting. Gentler and more rational approaches to discipline keep the child's arousal at a manageable level, with the result that the child is more likely to take in and remember the content of parental expectations. … The child who is regularly hurt via spanking or slapping tends to focus on avoiding punishment rather than understanding why a certain behavior is wrong.[3]

If our discipline approach scares our child, he's more focused on his fear and anxiety than on whatever lesson we're trying to impart. In the short term, this child might obey, but only because he's scared, not because he's learned anything. Over time, many children who are disciplined with harsh methods build up a defensive resistance to their parents. They might comply with their parent's rules initially, but they become increasingly sneaky and resentful, and eventually defiant.

Some of your friends might point out how well their adult children turned out even though they spanked, threatened, and yelled at them when they were young. It's true. Some children will grow up and be okay even if their parents use harsh forms of discipline like those Davies warns against. However, those kids likely turn out okay not *because* of the discipline, but *despite* it. Other protective factors can shield us from the long-term damage caused by mistreatment, and we can experience healing in adulthood through other relationships and therapeutic intervention. Frankly, some adults only appear okay. They're basically functional on the surface, but they carry wounds that prevent them from living vibrantly and to their full potential, especially within their closest relationships. The fact is, there's no good reason to use harsh discipline methods. It's our responsibility to manage the chaos that comes with immaturity, but we have to do it in a way that protects a child's attachment to us and protects his heart.

If we have a warm, respectful relationship with our child, he'll be more likely to see our limits, rules, and values as something worth paying attention to, and then we can guide him toward maturity. Of course, our emotional limitations and past experiences occasionally drive how we react in stressful situations. Despite my own ideals, sometimes I've been too hard on my kids. So I say all this with humility and without judgment toward you — no matter what you've done or what sort of discipline techniques you've used in the past. No matter how we got here, well, here we are together. Despite our shortcomings, we can begin thinking long-term. We can work toward an approach that will protect our children emotionally while we figure out how to address those problem behaviors.

Emotions 101: Emotions and the Good Life
As a first step toward maturity, it's important that our children gradually grow comfortable with the full array of their emotions, because their emotions help them become integrated human beings. Emotions aren't something to fear, avoid, or eradicate. They give power to our moral lives. One of our chief jobs as parents is to help our children grow to a place where they can control their emotional outbursts, but this will happen over time, and only with lots of support. To get to that

place, we have to help them gradually live with big feelings such as anger, fear, jealousy, or sadness, because they need all their feelings if they're going to arrive one day at true maturation and well-being.

Unfortunately, many of us grew up with confusing or even damaging messages about emotions, so we may struggle to understand our children's emotions. We enjoy it when they're being lovey-dovey and funny, but when they're expressing "negative" emotions, we're uncomfortable or even annoyed. Because kids lack self-mastery, their hard emotions like anger seem to go from zero to ten in a matter of seconds, often over trivial events. This drives us crazy, and our own emotions get caught up in their intensity, especially when we're in a hurry or tired.

When I was a young mom, I too often sent unhelpful signals to my kids about their feelings. In particular, I believed on some level that anger was an emotion we should all avoid, even though I knew logically it was natural to be angry sometimes. I wasn't comfortable experiencing my own anger, and I was anxious when others expressed anger around me. I also felt alarmed by sadness in my children. I believed that if my child was sad, I had failed in some way as a mom. I believed this for a long time, probably until my youngest was a toddler. Those were the two feelings I had a hard time witnessing in my kids: anger and sadness. I wanted to fix those emotions right away, to tidy them up and tuck them away. I didn't provide the support my kids needed to experience those emotions fully, and this meant they never moved through those feelings to the other side of them. I was inadvertently teaching them to go around the emotion or to pretend like the emotion didn't exist.

Thomas Aquinas on the Emotions

Saint Thomas Aquinas, thirteenth-century philosopher-theologian, offered me some clarity about what I needed to do as a mom to raise emotionally healthy kids. In his *Treatise on the Emotions*, Aquinas teaches that, on its own, any emotion is morally neutral.[4] Emotions are just something that happen to us, like an itch or the hiccup.[5] In contrast to some philosophers and theologians who view the emotions as inner drives that must be eradicated from the moral and spiritual life,[6] Aquinas grasps how all emotions play a necessary part in human flourishing.

God created us with emotions, so they must have some purpose. We're not meant to be disintegrated — with our internal, emotional stirrings cut off from our decision-making or our actions. From Aquinas's perspective, the emotions can assist our rational mind in exercising our will in cooperation with grace to achieve the true end that God has planned for us. Thinking needs the energy of emotions, and emotions need the discipline of the rational mind, as we strive to live morally upright lives. The mind and emotions are like two motors working together to move us forward on our path toward virtue and perfection.

Cultivating and Educating the Emotions

Of course, although emotions in themselves are morally neutral, how we express these emotions can be either virtuous or sinful. Feelings do not necessarily reflect reality, and if left unchecked they can lead us to vice. If we allow every emotional impulse to guide our actions, we won't grow up or have very many friends! Emotions shouldn't be quashed or ignored, but they do need to be cultivated, educated, and refined so we can act virtuously in response to them.[7] This becomes possible when we grow to a place where our emotions and our reason work in concert. The emotions must be tempered by reason; this is how the emotions become rightly ordered.

That's what makes our kids' outbursts so hard to take: Their emotions are not very well-ordered. But your child's fiery spirit now is a hint of the magnanimous person he may become one day. When rightly ordered, our emotions can move us to act rationally with great virtue and joy. The emotions are grace-filled pistons of holy action: Even intense emotions can lead to virtuous acts. Think of Martin Luther King Jr., filled with righteous anger when he delivered his "I Have a Dream" speech. His anger is what gave power to that rational, eloquent speech. Of course, anger can also give power to an abusive tirade. A wise person knows when to allow anger to fuel his actions toward a good cause, and he also knows when it's time to cool off or hold his tongue.[8] King knew it was time to do something with his anger, and we'll never forget it.

God can work through our emotions to guide us in our decision-making, but only if we're in a state of grace and only if we have a well-developed moral conscience. We can rely only on moral standards that are rooted in objective truth, not the yawning chasm of human opinion and impulses. When God becomes our compass, when we become free to follow his lead about what is good and true, our decisions will become more rational, because our decisions will increasingly reflect transcendent reality. Through grace, the emotions can aid our minds in making good decisions based on reality about ourselves and the world. Emotionally healthy people tend to know in their gut that an option is right or wrong, wise or imprudent, because they have a well-formed moral radar that is fine-tuned by their intellects and emotions. People who ignore their emotions often have a hard time making decisions, even if they're morally upright individuals. They weigh the pros and cons until they're blue in the face, and still they can't decide. People with avoidant attachment often have this problem. At the other end of the spectrum, people with ambivalent attachment tend to change their minds a lot because they don't trust their feelings. In these people, the mind and emotions are not working together.[9]

In short, our feelings can help us do the right thing, for the right reason, at the right time when reason and emotion live together comfortably in our lives. As our children mature, they become capable of this beautiful integration between the emotions, the rational mind, and the will. But when they're little, they're a bundle of emotions with nary a glimmer of rationality. If we don't recognize that all their emotions are normal and healthy, we may say or do things to disapprove of particular emotions or even punish our children for feeling them. We want our children to become more rational and self-controlled, but not at the cost of their emotional health and flourishing.

Emotions and the Good Life

Every healthy human being experiences fear, anger, sorrow, and disappointment. If our child grows up sensing these emotions are unacceptable to us, he'll learn to tune them out or stuff them down. But those emotions don't disappear. They are still sitting there in his gut — ignored, unprocessed, and unexpressed. Not only will he never learn how to handle such feelings in a socially acceptable way, but he'll also feel fragmented and emotionally flat. When he does express those feelings, they'll explode out in destructive ways to himself or those around him.

While I have more growing to do, I see clearly now that the emotions are a key to living the good life. The good life is filled with color, laughter, wonder, and joy, but also fear, anger, disgust, and sadness. That is where many of us were misled as children. We were made to feel that only happy, bubbly children are lovable. Sometimes our lovable children will be royally peeved or grossed out. We're okay with this, because we now know that only through the integration of their emotions into their overall pursuit of moral excellence will our kids be fully alive.

Sometimes in the heat of the moment, you just want your child to calm down and act sanely. But as you respond to him, remember that the underlying emotion and even his intentions are probably very good. Some of your child's most hair-raising behavior is rooted in a quality that is praiseworthy — a character trait you really want to protect because you'll admire it in the future. It might even lay the paving stones on his path to sainthood! It's simply the disordered way he's expressing himself right now that's bothersome. Parents are pressured to rush their kids through childhood to maturity, but maturity takes time and patience. There are many perfectly behaved grown-ups walking around who are only half alive because they don't feel anything. Childhood is messy and chaotic, but if you're seeing the chaos, you can learn to understand it and bring it to order and rest. What's tragic is when parents don't see their child's inner chaos because the child has learned to hide it in fear or shame. So when you see the chaos, you're doing something right!

Now then, how do Catholic parents preserve their children's emotional vitality while teaching them gradually how to live virtuously? We can get to the root of the behavior and M.E.N.D. the problem.

Getting to the Root of Misbehavior

Discipline advice from parenting experts too often focuses on a child's behavior and, more specifically, what the parent can do to the child to change the behavior without considering the child's emotional and cognitive development, or even her intentions. I do want to stop annoying, disruptive, or socially objectionable behavior, but mostly I want to empower my kids to make good choices for the right reasons. Because of this, I like to pay attention to what developmental psychology has to say about kids. The developmentalist tries to understand how children's cognitive and emotional development affects their behavior, including their moral choices and capacity for relationship. The developmentalist asks the same questions I'm asking myself as a parent:

- What does my child need to flourish, to mature into a vibrant, fully functioning adult? And what gets in the way of that flourishing?

- What are the feelings, needs, and motivations driving my child's behavior? What developmental limitations might explain the behavior?
- How can I handle a behavioral problem so that my child's heart remains whole while I help her along her way toward social, emotional, and spiritual maturity?

The developmentalist asks *why* before prescribing the *what*. As parenting expert Sarah Ockwell-Smith puts it: "Any discipline that focuses solely on 'the solution' actually disempowers you as a parent. Remember that a good teacher has a good understanding of their subject, and to achieve this they must first take the place of the student. Understanding the reasons for your child's undesirable behavior is the starting point for knowing how to improve it."[10]

Any time we try to fix a problem without understanding the cause of the problem, we'll merely be grasping in the dark at solutions. I'm giving you the information I wish I had when I became a mom two decades ago. As I gained greater insight into the causes of my children's behavior, I could avoid common triggers, and I finally recognized that what I was looking at in them was immaturity, not badness. Why is this so important? Because when we become wiser parents, we become more patient parents. We can white-knuckle through the morning trying with all our will power not to scream at our kids, but when we become wise parents, patience comes more naturally. When we understand our kids — what makes them tick, what challenges they're facing — we're less likely to take their behavior personally or to absorb their emotional energy. We're able to stay in control and become a strong leader for our children.

M.E.N.D.: Four Steps to Effective Discipline

The following are four steps to addressing behavioral problems in your home. I'll give you the *why* before I give you the *what*. The first three steps deal with understanding the reasons behind common behavioral issues in children so you can avoid triggers. Of course, sometimes you can't identify the cause of your child's behavior or you can't avoid a trigger, so the fourth step in M.E.N.D. offers attachment-safe, developmentally appropriate discipline strategies to steer your child toward more virtuous choices.

The four steps to effective discipline are:

1. **Modeling:** Does your child have appropriate and healthy modeling for his behavior? Is he picking up a bad habit from another child ... or a parent?
2. **Expectations:** Are your expectations appropriate for your child given his age and development?
3. **Need:** Is your child trying to get a legitimate need met with his behavior?
4. **Discipleship:** What attachment-safe discipline tool can you use to correct his behavior when the cause is unknown or the trigger is unavoidable? What can he learn from the experience?

MODELING (Who's my child following?)

The first thing we want to do when dealing with an inappropriate behavior is to ask ourselves whether the child learned it from somebody else. Sometimes we don't realize that our children are picking up on our own bad habits. They take their cues from us about how to act (and even feel) in response to annoying, frightening, or sad experiences. Consciously and unconsciously, they notice when we're rude to our spouse, gossip with our friends, or curse at other drivers. They are particularly likely to treat others the way we treat them. We can try to teach our children how to behave like civilized persons, but our lessons will go to waste if we aren't meeting our own expectations.

When my daughter Claire was about twelve, we went through a very uncomfortable period with her. Once a carefree, happy child, as a tween she had become irritable and sometimes a little hostile. When she was unhappy with one of us in the family, she tended to exit the room in a fury, stomp down the hallway, and slam her bedroom door behind her. Not fun. Everyone becomes angry on occasion, but there are acceptable ways to express it, and this wasn't one of them. The issue was partly that noxious combination of immaturity and hormones, but I know she was handling her anger the way she had seen me handle my own.

As I've shared, I didn't understand until many years into my mothering vocation how important all the emotions are for human well-being, so I tended to act like nothing bothered me. But plenty of things did bother me. Of course things bothered me. I couldn't admit it to myself, because I thought it was morally wrong to be angry or irritated. Yet emotions don't go away because you pretend they're not there, so every now and then something would set me off and the emotions would blast out. These eruptions tended to occur in interactions with my husband and not my children, but they were around sometimes. I'd huff around, and I occasionally slammed a door (or two) to vent. My stomping and slamming show was always followed by regret. I was having nothing more than an adult temper tantrum (which makes me feel quite sympathetic toward toddlers who have them). Although I always apologized for my "momtrums," my children still witnessed my behavior. I wasn't modeling for them how a mature person handles it when she's upset with another person.

When Claire was angry, she was drawing on my example; she was dealing with her emotions the way I dealt with mine. If you have a twelve-year-old, you're probably thinking, "What? That seems like typical twelve-year-old behavior to

me," and of course you're right. A twelve-year-old is still a little kid with grown-up hormones sparking in her brain. Still,
I was a bad example to her, which only added fuel to the fire.
I guess slamming doors is better than some alternatives, but I
wanted her to develop better coping skills. On the upside, at
least Claire was expressing her frustration in some way. If she
expressed it, I could help her manage it and communicate it in
a way that protected her relationships. But I needed to start by
being a good model for her. I've grown up along with my kids,
and I'm now better able to communicate the right message to
my kids when I'm upset. The message I want to communicate?
I'm angry. I'm disappointed. I'm hurt. But I'm in control and
I still love you. We'll work it out. We're in this together. That's
what I want to communicate. That's the example I want to set.

By sharing our feelings, but also remaining in control and
treating others around us with dignity, we're writing a script
in our kids' minds about how to act when they're feeling the
same way. Of course, every parent has bad days when they fall
off the good-example wagon. As long as these stumbles are an
exception in our homes, and not the rule, we can grow from
them. As disciple-parents, we know these stumbles provide
opportunities for us to grow as Christians, and to show our
children an example of humility, honesty, and reconciliation.

When Peer Orientation Sabotages Discipline

Children can pick up behavior problems and bad manners
from anybody they're around, not just their parents. If your
child picks up a bad habit or behavior from a friend, he'll respond quickly to your gentle redirection if he's securely attached to you. A problem arises, however, when a child depends on a peer to get his attachment needs met. It's called
peer orientation. Many loving, well-meaning parents are
blindsided by it. Dr. Gordon Neufeld has studied this phenomenon through a cross-disciplinary lens for many years.[11] Peer
orientation happens when children emotionally orbit around

each other rather than their parents and other adults who are responsible for them. Understand that peer *attachment* and peer *orientation* are different. Peer attachment is very natural in our children: It's very exciting to be with people who are like them. Peer orientation, on the other hand, is damaging and unnatural because it pulls the children toward their peers at the same time that they are no longer moved to attach to their parents. A peer-oriented child turns to her peers for the answer to her yearning for closeness, sameness, belonging, and significance, while at the same time moving away from her parents to be the answer to these needs. This doesn't work, because children aren't meant to be responsible for meeting one another's needs.

Peer orientation has become an increasing problem in our culture, and it's believed to be at the root of many psychological problems in today's youth, including bullying, anxiety, superficiality, and a failure to launch successfully into adulthood. Peer orientation is a uniquely modern phenomenon. In the mid-twentieth century, as family ties weakened, "youth culture" (which did not exist one hundred years ago) became increasingly accepted as normal. Throughout history, culture, traditions, faith, and even vocabulary were transmitted vertically, from generation to generation. Now they're transmitted horizontally, kid to kid. Parents are led to believe that this is healthy, but it isn't. As Neufeld stresses, just because something is normal (common) does not mean it's natural or healthy.[12]

Nobody is suggesting that our children shouldn't have friends. Of course, friendships are great for our kids. Playing and exploring an interest with a friend is fun and a wonderful opportunity for kids to practice social skills. But our children should be learning most social skills from their grown-ups. They shouldn't care more about what their friends think of them than they do about what we think, and they shouldn't be depending on their peers to fulfill their attachment needs. In healthy development, a child's primary attachment figures are her parents, until that source of security is replaced not by a peer, but by her emerging sense of self. A peer-oriented child looks to peers for her sense of identity, for emotional support, and for messages about what's acceptable, good, and desirable in the world. The context for raising our children is sabotaged by peer orientation. We lose our power to parent, because we've lost our children's hearts. The peer-oriented child doesn't really care much what we say or do, so we can't guide her. She's often filled with counterwill, resisting our guidance over even small matters, so it's nearly impossible to discipline her effectively, unless we resort to increasingly severe threats and punishments. Even if she responds to these threats and punishments, it's usually only because she wants to get us "off her back," and not because she cares about us or the lesson we're trying to communicate. As the problem becomes more serious, the peer-oriented child may try to dominate us by taking the lead in setting rules and making plans. She may become bossy, prescriptive, and demand that we give her what she deserves. Very unpleasant.

This issue of peer orientation is germane to many topics I explore in this book. Such kids are harder to teach and parent, and they lack a compass point through which to transmit culture, faith, and moral values. Peer-oriented kids aren't looking to their parents for anything like culture, faith, or values. It's not meant to be this way.

Collecting a Peer-Oriented Child

If you suspect that your child is peer-oriented, the first order of the day is to "collect" (or win back) your child. There's no point correcting the behavior yet; it'll just turn into a power struggle. You can't order your child to attach to you; you have to lead her to it.

1. Work the attachment. Ensure she knows how much you

adore her, how much you delight in her company, how much she can count on you. Don't tell her this. *Show her.* Through the six ways of attaching that we explored in chapter 1, you can regain a child's trust and win back her heart. You will have to cut down on exposure to the problem role model. This will take commitment and time, and your child won't like it. If she is extremely attached to the peer and lacks any sense of connection to you, reduce the exposure gradually. Slowly increase her connection to you while you decrease exposure to the peer.

When your child needs to be collected, don't inform her of this. Just *become* what she needs without any announcement about it. Focus on the things in your relationship that are working and awaken her attachment to you by finding more ways to connect.

2. Create scenarios of dependence.[13] Arrange activities in which you are clearly in the lead, and your child needs to depend on you. This might be something simple, like teaching her how to sew an apron or build a birdhouse. You can also take your child outside her comfort zone, like traveling to an unfamiliar place.

Dr. Neufeld tells a beautiful story in his book about collecting his teenage daughter Tasha, who had become peer-oriented.[14] He rented a cottage out in the country, far from home. At first Tasha was sullen and complained of boredom because "nobody" was around. (You see, when your child is peer-oriented, you count as a "nobody.") Gradually she accepted his companionship on walks and for canoeing. Then, they naturally started cooking together every night, and conversations unfolded. By the end of the trip, she didn't want to leave! He'd collected her heart. After that, they shared daily and weekly rituals to preserve their connection.

3. Don't appear weak or overwhelmed in your parenting role. Your child has to have a sense that you have the relationship under control; if a peer-attached child thinks you're in over your head, she will try to take charge or turn to a peer for leadership. Engage warmly but stand confidently as the leader in the relationship. Deep down your child wants you to take the lead. You might encounter back-talk, resistance, and tears from her in the beginning, but once you've collected her, you'll become your child's compass point again.

Don't let anybody make you feel guilty for prioritizing your connection to your children. Kids want to be held close. If we don't lead, gather, and hold our kids close, they will look for somebody else to do it. So hold on to your kids!

Preventing Peer Orientation in Healthy Kids

You might be wondering how you can avoid peer orientation in a child who is securely attached to you, but who also enjoys peer friendships. To avoid peer orientation, ensure you remain the go-to person for your child when she has a question or problem, and ensure you're the answer to her attachment yearnings. In fact, you'll discover that when you *are* the answer to her attachment yearnings, you don't need to *have* all the answers to her problems. So be the answer to her deep desire to draw close to, to belong to, to matter to, to be loved, to be heard. Your child needs to know you are her best bet for getting her needs met. As Dr. Neufeld puts it, "We need to give children something to grasp, something to hold dear, something they can take to heart and not want to let go of. Whatever we provide must come from us or be ours to give. And whatever we give our children, the key is that in holding on to it, they will be holding on to us."[15] Without this connection to you, your child will not only pick up bad fashion tips from her friends, but she'll start adopting their moral values, political views, and religious beliefs (or lack thereof).

Dr. Neufeld recommends that parents deemphasize peer relationships throughout childhood.[16] This advice applies for all children, not only peer-oriented children. Your child's emotional, social, and spiritual world should orbit around you and your family, not her friends. Healthy children enjoy friendships, but they don't need to spend every waking minute with their friends. How much time is appropriate? It depends on your child and the friend. Children younger than five really don't need to have peer socialization without you around. They aren't capable of the personal integration that's necessary for healthy peer socializing.

For older kids, a clue that a child is ready for peer socialization is when she can hold on to her sense of self while mixing with her peers. This is part of the integrative process: Healthy development allows us to experience togetherness and community without losing ourselves.[17] It's the way God meant for us to live, and it's a magnificent gift. But this takes a lot of maturity; some adults never develop this capacity. If your child cannot maintain her own feelings, values, and boundaries when she's in a peer group or with a friend, she's not ready. If your child comes home talking and acting like a friend, and begins resisting your parenting, then she's not ready. Until she finds her sense of self, she needs to be able to hold on to you. So be her answer. You're her best bet until she grows up. This doesn't mean you shouldn't allow her to hang out with friends, but you have to take responsibility and pay attention to her reactions. Sometimes you just need to reduce the exposure or ensure you're around during peer socializing.

As she matures, ensure your child has healthy relationships with many trusted adult role models: grandparents, aunts, uncles, clergy, youth group leaders, and teachers. Along with your role modeling, these adults are the best agents of healthy socialization and moral development.

When Technology Sabotages Real Relationships
Children can become superficially attached to substitutes for real relationships, including gaming, social media, or other electronic devices. They become increasingly isolated and

moody, and they may become reactive when parents limit or remove access to their devices.[18] This can happen even in warm, loving homes. The creators of interactive games and social media platforms are becoming increasingly shrewd about using what we know about child and adolescent psychology to lure in and grip our children's attention, no matter how bad it is for their emotional and psychological health. If you suspect this is an issue in your child's life, it's time to scale back access to technology. A tech-saturated kid might think she's dying when her devices are removed, but assure her that there is no proven link between technology abstinence and mortality!

EXPECTATIONS (Am I expecting too much?)

Sometimes what* we consider "inappropriate" behavior is completely appropriate for our child given his age and development. Sometimes we might expect more of our children than they can possibly handle. We take our three-year-old to a wedding reception where she's expected to eat crudités from fine china, and we're embarrassed when she sits under the table screaming for a chicken nugget. Or we introduce our child to her new sibling, and we're shocked when she says the baby looks like a fish and we should send "it" back. Before we pounce on our child for such behavior, it's helpful to understand how emotional and cognitive development unfold in children.

Young kids do things no rational person would do. And that's the problem. They aren't rational. Their behavior is erratic, and they make bad choices without thinking through the consequences. Children are born with a potential for self-control, self-reflection, and follow-through, but these qualities emerge over many years, and only if children are given the freedom to mature in the way God designed. As I've said before, maturity is possible and desirable, but not inevitable. We deal with adults daily who have never really matured. So, let's give our kids a chance to grow up.

Children have "jobs" they're working on at each stage of their childhoods. If we allow them to do these jobs, they'll have an easier time navigating the challenges they encounter at later stages, and they'll develop specific virtues (or character strengths) that will serve them well for the rest of their lives.[19] Here's an overview of these stages and their accompanying virtues:

Infancy: Most of your newborn's brain development occurs after birth. Newborns have nearly 200 billion brain cells, but very few connections between the cells in the higher brain.[20] Your newborn's brain is very open to sculpting by both positive and negative experiences. The brainstem is the most developed part of her brain; it controls her reflexes (sucking, crying), and it works with the amygdala to handle her emotional systems (including rage, fear, and separation). Infants need their parents' help to calm down when one of these emotional systems is triggered. When she's supported consistently, over time she develops connections in the frontal lobes of the brain that will help her calm down on her own. Your infant's job is to learn to trust you; from this place of trust she is able to explore the world through her senses. She is developing the virtue of trust.

Toddlers (one to three years): During these years, your child's brain builds seven hundred new neural connections ... every second.[21] Incredible! However, the higher brain, which is responsible for self-regulation and rationality, will remain immature for many years. Your child is very egocentric: He focuses almost exclusively on his own needs and point of view. He's beginning to internalize your values and standards, and he internalizes and mirrors your way of handling stress. One of your child's primary developmental tasks is to explore his independence and exercise his will, so he will naturally test limits and boundaries. His growing autonomy can also trigger separation anxiety: It's like he takes a step away from you, but then needs to look back to ensure you're there. Through confronting the challenges of this stage, he's developing the virtue of perseverance.

Preschoolers (three to five years): Your child's higher brain is still undeveloped. She operates mostly from the lower brain, which is responsible for the fight-or-flight response and the emotions. When distressed, she can't use reasoning and self-talk to calm herself down like a teenager or adult can. She's impulsive, and quite reactive and emotionally charged when she's upset. On the upside, she's growing more comfortable with new situations because she can categorize her experiences better. So your preschooler will be less "clingy" when meeting new people or in a new environment. During these years, she uses play as a means to explore reality. As she takes on the developmental tasks of this stage, she's developing the virtue of curiosity.

Early childhood (five to eight years): An important cognitive milestone comes in early childhood: Your child develops the ability to reflect on her own thoughts and to consider the direct consequences of her choices. So, for example, she might become angry and want to hit her sister, but she has second thoughts because she loves her sister and knows it's wrong to hit. This is called the "5 to 7 shift," because this capacity to second-guess herself usually happens between five and seven years old, give or take.[22] Because of this shift, your child begins to develop self-regulation, but she still needs your support in managing her emotions and making good choices. By eight years old, she will begin taking more initiative in starting and exploring her own projects, and her moral conscience is emerging. When she falls short of her own expectations, she can become very frustrated. If all goes well, she will develop the virtue of self-control and the character strength of competence.

Middle childhood (eight to twelve years): During this stage, the frontal lobe, which is responsible for problem-solving and categorizing, matures in your child's brain. However, his prefrontal cortex (which covers the front part of the frontal lobe) is still immature. This means your child is capable of more abstract thought, but he can still have a hard time expressing his emotions responsibly. He's learning to follow through on the projects he plans and the commitments he makes. He'll need your encouragement and support, but by the end of this stage he should be able to set goals and meet them. Your child is developing the virtue of prudence.

Adolescence (thirteen to eighteen years): In the adolescent years, your child's prefrontal cortex matures. The prefrontal cortex is responsible for "executive function," which allows him to think about the consequences of his choices in a very sophisticated way. He can consider the good and bad aspects of his choices, and then moderate his behavior or set goals after reflecting on these choices. So a teenager does have increased emotional regulation and impulse control, especially compared to his younger siblings. However, his brain won't be fully developed until he's in his midtwenties. Teenagers often experience a flooding of emotion that overwhelms them, so they may be reactive in stressful situations. They may engage in risky behavior because they aren't very good at assessing risks; your input is critical for helping them make safe choices. In the teen years, your child is working on identifying the values by which he wants to live; his self-identity is emerging. If all goes well, he will develop the virtues of integrity and courage.

We can see how our own adult perspective and expectations can clash with our child's attempts to practice the developmental skills they're preoccupied with at these different stages. For example, the toddler needs to learn to exercise his will in a responsible way, but his initial efforts are usually pretty sloppy, especially when coupled with his lack of self-control. But we don't want to crush the will while trying to deal with the emotional outbursts. The will is a gift even though the child doesn't have a handle on it yet. And recognizing the process of brain development during childhood reveals clearly why it's unrealistic to expect a toddler to have consistent self-control or to expect her to think about the consequences of her choices in a time-out. Our children's attempts to navigate these developmental milestones can be frustrating at times, but they are almost always doing the best they can, especially given their emotional, cognitive, and physical limitations. Sometimes a toddler really can't handle the peas sitting too close to the potatoes; sometimes an eight-year-old really can't sit at his desk without fidgeting; sometimes a twelve-year-old really can't express her anger without slamming her door. They can't do these things yet, but they are on their way if we support them and show them the way.

This doesn't mean we excuse inappropriate behavior. But I think it does mean our children don't deserve punishment for being immature. It's unfair to expect a child to behave like an adult and then to punish him when he doesn't. It's merciful to recognize his limitations, and then guide him toward maturity. We can empathize with our children's emotional outbursts and poor choices when we understand their developmental limitations. From there, we can gently guide our children in understanding appropriate ways to express their feelings, and how to make amends when their actions hurt somebody.

Scripting Maturity

When we anticipate a situation that we know will require more maturity than a child can handle, sometimes we can intervene by scripting for the child what to do. For example, we can script how to be a big brother, how to hold a baby, how to pet a dog, or how to sit at Mass. We're scripting behavior that would happen spontaneously if the child were more mature. We take the lead and show him how to do it. Most of us do this without thinking about it, because we know intuitively that we can mentor our children regarding what mature behavior looks like, even when they're immature.

Scripting is especially helpful before high-stakes events.

Say you're going to that wedding where your child will be served crudités on fine china. Rehearse with your child well before the event: Let her know what she'll see and how people will be dressed, seated, and behaving. Explain to her that at weddings little girls feel very fancy, like a princess sipping from a shiny teacup with a pinky in the air. Let her practice by having a tea party with her. Then, when you're at the wedding you can say to her, "Oh, goody, you get to be a princess at a party now. You and I will sit together on our chairs and practice our very best princess manners."

Though a child might be too immature to be a good big brother all the time, pet the dog correctly all the time, or sit still through an entire wedding reception, scripting is very helpful for bridging the period between immaturity and maturity. It gives the child an idea what's expected of him, and a chance to practice it, even if he can't do it perfectly.

NEED (Does my child have an unmet need?)

Sometimes when a child is misbehaving, she's simply trying to get a need met, however feckless her approach. First, ensure your child's physical needs for food, sleep, and safety are met. If she's tired, hungry, or hurt, she has a reduced capacity to manage her emotions and reactions. We all know babies and toddlers need plenty of sleep, but let's not overlook the impact of sleep deprivation on our older children's ability to cope with stress. Teenagers are often expected to function with far less sleep than they need. If you're sure these physical needs are met, ask yourself whether her needs for connection, stimulation, and certainty have been met. These are some basic psychological hungers, which all must be satisfied and in balance for optimal mental and physical health.[23] Your child's misbehavior might be a signal that one of these needs is not being met or is out of balance. Sometimes she's getting too much of one thing and is lacking in another.

Connection: Misbehavior is often the first sign that our child's attachment tank is empty or running low. It's our job to hold our children close in attachment; they shouldn't have to work for it. So if your child is whining, clinging, or pestering, think through the six phases of attachment (physical proximity, sameness, belonging, significance, love, and being known). Your child might be thirsting for physical closeness or for reminders about how special she is to you. When a child's attachment tank is full, she transitions naturally to exploring and playing, and then mom or dad can focus on grown-up tasks. Sometimes when we're preoccupied, it's easy to tune our kids out, but in the long run our homes will be more peaceful, and we'll get more done, if we attend to those needs before our kids ring their attachment alarm bells.

Stimulation: Our children won't go off exploring and trying new things if their attachment alarm is sounding, but if you know those needs are satiated, ask yourself whether your child might be bored. All human beings need to feel energized and vital, including our kids. We all need some spontaneity and novelty in our lives sometimes. Boredom, of course, can lead to creativity and exploration, but sometimes small children don't know they're bored. They feel agitated, but they don't know they need to find something new to do. I'm not suggesting parents entertain their children around the clock, but we can help them out of a funk or rut. Children do need to learn to play alone, but sometimes they need a gentle suggestion or invitation to try something new.

Children can also become *overstimulated*. Some situations are just too overwhelming for some kids — too loud, bright, or crowded. If you have a very sensitive child, you're probably already attuned to his tolerance levels. My son Dominic can't handle loud places for long periods of time. In particular, crowded arcade-type environments with lots of flashing lights and screaming children overwhelm him quickly. He doesn't even like bowling for more than thirty minutes, because the crashing of the pins is too much for him. It doesn't mean I never allow him to visit such venues, but I've learned to understand his limits. We can also teach our sensitive children to recognize the signals in their bodies that they're becoming overwhelmed. This self-knowledge empowers them to speak up for themselves when they need a break.

Certainty: Finally, all human beings need to know what the rules are and who's in charge. I've already explained the importance of having rules and expectations that are *reasonable* for our children's age and development. We should also ensure our rules and expectations are very *clear* to our kids. Reasonable and clear rules will prevent many, many discipline problems. Kids like to know what we expect of them — it makes them feel more secure. Sometimes we think our kids know what we expect, but they don't. They may need reminders or visual cues to help them remember.

If you've never had official rules in your home, it's never too late to start. Rules fall into different categories: There are rules for morality (no cursing, attend Mass with the family on Sundays), safety (no running in the house), hygiene (brush your teeth before bed), proper manners (say please, don't interrupt mom when she's talking), home care (cleaning, decluttering, garden care), and the stretching of independence (curfews, bedtimes). It's especially important to have clear rules about how your family treats one another (be kind, no hitting). These rules help you redirect your kids when they start arguing.

Catholic social doctrine teaches us that in order to foster a spirit of cooperation and participation, communities need the input and contributions of all people at every level of society.[24] I think this principle can help us introduce a little creativity into our family rule-making. Now let me say right off the bat, I believe parents should be the rule-and boundary-setters in the home. However, as children mature, and to the extent appropriate for them, we can include them in creating and negotiating some household rules. The point of doing this is to give them practice in self-expression, fairness, and cordial debate. Of course, some rules, such as those relating to morality, are nonnegotiable, but others, like bedtimes and chore assignments, can be negotiated. Kids feel appreciated and respected when we include them this way.

We also need to practice the virtues of courage and perseverance in enforcing our rules. This is a problem area in my parenting. I can become a little wobbly on enforcing my household and behavioral rules, usually because I don't want to ruffle my kids' feathers. Big mistake. I've learned that if I'm inconsistent with enforcing rules and expectations, my children assume there aren't any. This leads to conflict with them anyway! Feathers need to be ruffled sometimes. When I enforce rules and boundaries, my kids have confidence that I'm in charge and that I actually know what I'm doing.

Our kids also experience certainty through predictable routines and daily rhythms. Some parents like to "go with the flow" and take the day as it comes, but children like to know what to expect. At the other extreme, some parents might control a child's day too much, not allowing her any kind of freedom. This can be a huge trigger for toddlers and preschoolers whose clothing, food, activities, bedtime, and even friends are often chosen by parents. Sometimes the only thing they can control is their behavior, so they shout, backchat, or whine. My advice: Choose your battles. It's okay to give your small kids some choices about what they wear, where they sit, what cup they use at the table, or which book to read at bedtime. By giving them some agency in limited areas of their life, you'll also affirm their emerging sense of autonomy.

When we think about it, even we adults have a harder time controlling our emotions and actions when one of these physical or psychological needs is unmet or out of balance. Much more so for children.

DISCIPLE (What can my child learn from this experience?)

We've covered some potential causes of misbehavior. When you provide healthy emotional modeling for your child, respect his developmental limitations, and recognize his needs, you'll discover that many behavioral issues are avoided entirely because you've avoided triggers. Sometimes, though, you just don't know why your child is misbehaving or you can't avoid a trigger. In these situations, you need some practical ideas for how you can respond when your child makes a mistake or is heading in that direction.

Having a conflict with your child isn't necessarily a sign that your connection with him is broken. When you keep your own cool and remain emotionally open, your strength keeps the connection strong. You become like a shepherd guiding a little lamb in the right direction on the safe path toward home. With your shepherd's staff of strength and calm, you can accompany your child through his hard feelings to the other side of them. There are many corrective yet gentle discipline tools that can help you in this shepherding work. Just as ancient shepherds used horns and special verbal calls to keep their flocks close and on the right path, you can use these discipline tools to guide your child in making better choices without demeaning her dignity or damaging his trust in you.

Virtue Training

No matter which discipline tool you use, virtue training should be part of it. Our children should know why the virtues are important for building character, and how to recognize virtue (and vice) in themselves and others. The more our kids exercise their virtue muscles, the stronger those muscles become and the easier it becomes to act virtuously.[25] Striving for virtue transforms not only our children's actions, but also their hearts. They'll not only act nobly, but they'll become truly, deeply noble. The great spiritual masters tell us that the more virtuous a person is, the more liberated and authentically beautiful he is. If our children become deeply rooted in virtue, they'll become progressively free from egocentrism and less attracted to anything that will lead them away from God.[26]

Some important virtues you might include in your virtue training:[27] compassion, courage, cooperation, courtesy, eutrapelia (lightheartedness), fidelity, gratitude, generosity, humility, honesty, hospitality, joy, justice (giving to others their due), kindness, love, loyalty, mercy, patience, peacemaking, perseverance, prudence, respect, responsibility, self-control, and trustworthiness. Spend time reading stories with your kids that spark conversations about the virtues. After you watch a movie together, discuss the virtues demonstrated by or lacking in the characters. "Catch" your child practicing a virtue and mention it with delight. These activities will build your child's virtue vocabulary. In nurturing virtue in our kids, cultivating the emotions (as discussed above) is inseparable from intellectual instruction in how to identify particular virtues.[28] We don't want our kids to know the virtues like they memorize state capitals. We want them to become virtuous with rightly ordered emotions.

Virtue training not only stops problem behavior, but it works to change your child's perspective and his heart so he can make good choices on his own. He'll realize over time that we have to give up bad habits to acquire good ones, and that good habits liberate us to become who we're meant to be. Virtue training empowers your child to recognize the good and to seek it.

Do-Overs

This tool is helpful with children of all ages. I learned it from Greg and Lisa Popcak's book *Parenting with Grace*, and I've been using it for many years. A do-over is a quick interruption or redirection of a misstep your child makes. When your child speaks rudely, treats a sibling harshly, or displays rash behavior, ask her to try again. Correct her warmly and firmly with a prompt, "Ah, why don't you say that again a bit more politely" or "Please turn around and close that door again more gently." You are maintaining your connection to her while redirecting her behavior. In my own mothering, these redirections are often lighthearted, especially if I know the child is simply being absent-minded.

Cool-Off Time and Couch Time

Many parenting experts have become concerned about the overuse of time-outs and, in particular, the way time-outs tend to be used as jail time where the child is isolated away from the family. While he's "in jail," the child is asked to think about his behavior and about how he will do better in the future. The concern is twofold. First, most parents use time-outs with young kids who lack the ability to analyze their own behavior critically. This requires concrete thinking, which children won't develop until they're teenagers. Given his cognitive maturity, a little child isn't sitting in time-out contemplating his behavior and his future rehabilitation. He's just feeling crummy and maybe really mad at mean ol' mom or dad. Second, young kids experience isolation very differently from older kids. They can become truly distressed when separated from their parents. Kids may act out because they're seeking our attention; they want some kind of connection, even if it's negative. So the last thing they need is to be sent away from us.

If you share these concerns, or if you're just looking for more options to explore, a "cool-off" is a great alternative to a time-out. This tool can be used with kids of any age, but it's particularly helpful for toddlers and preschoolers. When your child's emotions are getting away from him, have a safe, comfortable place for your child to relax until he calms down. Present the cool-off spot as an opportunity, not a punishment. It should be comfortable and appealing — think pillows, books, cuddly toys, gentle music. I once had a cool-off spot inside a kiddy tent in my family room. Make a habit of encouraging a cool-off well before a situation explodes or your child becomes out of control. The earlier you catch the behavior, the easier it is to keep a child engaged with you so you can help him. He'll be able to hold on to your calm and control until he finds his own again.

I like this alternative to time-outs because you're giving your child strategies for coping with escalating emotions or charged situations. It also gives the *parent* a chance to collect her thoughts while the *child* has a break from the bothersome behavior. This reduces the likelihood that the parent will react in anger. We all need a break from conflict when our emotions are percolating. Modeling such breaks, and allowing our children to have them, is beneficial to them now and in their future relationships. When I'm in the middle of a conflict with one of my kids, if I know I'm losing my yearning for connection to them or losing my ability to put the relationship before the behavior (more on this below), I take a break before I say something I don't really mean.

If you think your child is trying to get attention with her behavior, Dr. Larry Cohen, author of *Playful Parenting*, suggests "couch time," a variation of the cool-off. Sit down on the couch *with* your child, snuggle up, and talk it over. Cohen explains that whatever the problem behavior might be, disconnection caused it, made it worse, or made the problem harder to solve. Either the child or the parent can call couch time, where you can talk about what's going on. Present the issue as a "we" problem rather than a "you" problem, so the child knows you're on the same team (attaching through loyalty).

The cool-off place and couch time provide a natural time and place to teach children how to express their emotions in a virtuous way, or when it's imprudent to express their emotions at all. Sometimes the best thing we can do is help our children tolerate the discomfort of an emotion until they move through it to the other side.

Logical Consequences

This tool should only be used when children are old enough to reflect on their choices, so about age seven and up. As they mature, we want our children to grow in wisdom, and this includes understanding that their choices will lead to specific outcomes. How they treat others, spend their time, and respond to rules will produce consequences for themselves and those around them. Imposing clear and consistent *logical* consequences for a child's poor choices can be part of the parental task of providing boundaries and safety. Consequences are nothing new. Spanking, grounding, and taking away toys and privileges are common consequences imposed on kids for misbehaving. But these consequences aren't connected logically to the child's actions, so the child experiences the consequence as an arbitrary punishment. Grounding a child for forgetting to do a chore is not logically connected. The consequence is a penalty, and that's all.

As a teaching tool, we can use *logical* consequences to guide and instruct the child's heart in virtue, and to correct the effect of his misstep. Discuss the specific virtues lacking in his choices and which virtues can help him make better choices next time. Help your child see what he can do to make the situation right. For example, the child who avoids doing assigned chores shows a lack of courtesy and responsibility. You could review what these virtues mean and how to practice them. A logical consequence might be that he isn't allowed to play outside until his chores are done. Another example: The child who breaks a lamp because he was throwing a ball in the house (which is against your rules) shows a lack of prudence, obedience, and respect. A logical consequence would be that the ball is put away for a few days, and you might require that he pays for the lamp out of his allowance.

I do think it's important that we recognize our children's positive intentions even when they mess up. The child who forgets to do her chores might be working on a sewing project and have lost track of time. We should try to see the positive intention behind the action, but that doesn't mean we excuse the behavior. "I know how easy it is to lose track of time when you're sewing, but we did agree that you'd vacuum the living room on Fridays." We can extend compassion while teaching virtue.

Problem-Solving

Problem-solving is one of the best tools you can use with older children and teens. It not only allows you to preserve your bond with your child while dealing with a behavioral issue, but it gives your child practice in considering the viewpoints of others and coming up with workable solutions that satisfy everyone. Children can grow frustrated or discouraged by ordinary relational conflict because they don't know how to make things better. With your guidance, they can develop valuable problem-solving skills that they will carry with them into adulthood.

Here are some problem-solving steps recommended by many conflict-management experts:

- **Define the problem**: Identify the specific problem and the underlying needs or fears of the people involved.
- **Brainstorm options**: Work with your child to identify different solutions to the problem. Accept all suggestions, no matter how wild!
- **Evaluate the options**: Now reflect on your solutions list and talk together about which ones would best resolve the problem while meeting the needs of everyone involved. If the problem is a biggie, help your child understand the importance of prayer and Christian discernment in evaluating choices.
- **Implement the solution**: After you've identified

the solution that satisfies your child, have her try
out the solution.

- **Evaluate whether the solution worked**: After
  your child has tried her solution, discuss whether
  it's working and whether she needs to revisit the
  brainstorming list.

Problem-solving exercises are helpful in many contexts: when
you have a disagreement with your child about something
she wants to do, when your child is having a conflict with a
friend or sibling, or even when your child is struggling with
a personal obstacle (how to complete her homework and still
attend ballet three times a week). I've described problem-solving
here as a formal process, but you can improvise and use
a more simplified approach depending on the situation and
your child's maturity.

Follow-Through and Physical Redirection

If your child is refusing to comply with your directions or
rules, sometimes you can help her along with a combination
of two tools: follow-through and physical redirection.[29] Follow-through
involves telling the child what the consequence
will be if she doesn't comply with the request or rule. Parents
need to follow through on what they say, with the fewer
words spoken the better. No yelling needed. We tell the
child clearly what the consequence will be: If she doesn't stop
running around the store, we're going to the car until she's
ready to comply; if she doesn't come to the bathroom for her
bath, you won't have time to play bathtub games with her.
Follow-through may sometimes require physical redirection.
Physical redirection involves taking the child gently but firmly
by the hand (or carrying her if she's very small) and taking her
where she needs to go.

Use the physical redirection approach very sparingly and
only for young children; it wouldn't be appropriate for an old-

er child or teenager. It should be used only if the attachment is secure between parent and child. Also, never aggressively force the child; you merely take her hand and walk her (or carry her) where she needs to go. Avoid using the physical redirection technique when you're angry. If necessary, have a cool-off or couch time.

I used physical redirection with my very small kids, but when possible I combined it with playful parenting.[30] I turned redirection into a game. For example, to get a stubborn preschooler to the dinner table I might say, "Did you see that? I think there's a frog under the table trying to eat our pasta!" Then I would take my child's hand and tell her we need to tiptoe very quietly and look under the table for the frog. "Is it there? Ah! I think I hear it!" Wanting the fun to continue, my child would nearly always follow my lead.

Here I've offered only a handful of general tips that might be helpful in a variety of situations. For many more tips and ideas for addressing specific behavioral issues, including potty training and sleep problems, my favorite discipline resources are *Parenting with Grace* by Greg and Lisa Popcak, *No Drama Discipline* by Daniel Siegal, and *Gentle Discipline* by Sarah Ockwell-Smith.

Merciful Ignoring

Sometimes behaviors are annoying to adults, but they are temporary, developmental behaviors. If the behavior isn't harmful to the child or others, we can consider just ignoring it. If we discipline or try to change every annoying behavior, we'll be very busy. It's okay to make a conscious decision that you won't engage in battles over small stuff. Kids might talk too loudly, play annoying games, or like wearing strange outfits. My middle two children sometimes glom on to annoying fads together that I basically ignore because I know they'll outgrow them. For a while they were "dabbing," but this bizarre arm movement has been replaced by flicking their leg up in

their air while saying "leg." Don't ask me why this is so entertaining, but they connect throughout the day by flicking and
laughing together. Maybe they're in a secret society of can-can
dancers. I know this too shall pass! By "ignore" I don't mean
you never say anything, but don't feel compelled to weed out
this kind of temporary behavior through discipline, even the
positive, gentle kind. Reserve your correction for bigger, more
worrisome behaviors.

The Relationship Is the Bottom Line

It's important that we never give our children the impression
that their behavior is bigger than our love for them. So even
when using these gentler discipline tools, we should never
make the behavior the bottom line; the relationship is the bottom line. Even when a child has done something shocking, we
want to resist any statements or ultimatums that might leave
the child with the impression that if he doesn't get it together,
the relationship will be damaged or severed. It's okay to point
out that the behavior is unacceptable and to correct the behavior through one of the discipline tools, but at some point,
make sure you remind your child that you're still his mom or
dad, and you still love him. Let him know you still want to be
with him, he still belongs with you, he's still significant to you.

The connection is the fundamental context through
which we guide our children; if that is broken, no guidance
will happen anyway. If you intuit that pursuing your agenda (virtue training and correcting your child's choices) will
jeopardize the relationship, consider backing off a little. Your
agenda is probably necessary and worthy, but sometimes it
doesn't work. If your discipline is just doing damage and tear-
ing the relationship apart, hit the pause button and work on
reestablishing the relationship. This is a dance that requires
intuition. In my own experience, this pause may be required
for only a few hours (for example, when the incident occurs
in a social setting with my child's peers around) or days (for

example, when emotions are running high and the discussion isn't productive). In one very serious situation with one of my children, I had to back off entirely for a few months; I first had to work on reestablishing trust between myself and my child. When I have to hit pause, I do tell my children we'll discuss things "later," and I let them know when that will be, so they know what to expect.

Welcoming Tears of Frustration

Your child may become upset when you create rules, limits, or consequences. She may even cry. This is not a sign that you're a bad parent or that you need to find a new parenting technique. It's a good sign. These are "the tears of futility," and they are healthy tears.[31] (The term *tears* here is figurative: A younger child might have actual tears, but older children may just express great sadness and disappointment.) Our children have to learn to live with frustration and disappointment. The reality is they can't have everything they want, when they want it. If we avoid every situation that would cause our children to experience this futility, they'll become controlling, and they won't develop healthy resilience.[32] There are necessary frustrations in life that lead our children to sadness, but when they let go, they grow from the experience. We're changed by the things we can't change. This is called the adaptive process, and it's critical for healthy maturation. Some children become chronically aggressive or controlling because they're stuck in the frustration and never get to the tears of acceptance. They cannot adapt to everyday losses and futilities.

We should support our kids through tough feelings, of course. I will talk more about emotion coaching in the next chapter on empathy, but here are some tips for handling your child's emotional outbursts. This advice applies to coaching a child through any kind of emotional upset, but it's particularly useful when he's upset about your rules and limits. Explain to your child that all feelings are okay, but if he wants to express those feelings to you, then he must do it appropriately.[33] Be very clear that rudeness, cruelty, or violence is unacceptable no matter how he feels. "It's okay to feel angry with Mommy, and it's okay to tell Mommy that you're angry, but it's never okay to spit at Mommy."

Give him practical ideas for what he can do with his feelings instead. Your suggestions will depend on his age and abilities, and note that different children respond to different outlets: some kids need to do something physical, while others need to relax. Look at what your child is doing when he gets frustrated or angry, and come up with healthy options. Sometimes kids like to express their emotions with their words — by talking to us, writing in a journal, or praying. Often, however, you'll discover your child needs to express those emotions in other ways, because he doesn't have the words or because this just isn't how he works. Maybe he could jump on a trampoline? Tear up a newspaper? Stomp on some bubble wrap? Throw some darts at a dart board? Run around the block? Dance? Play the piano? Knit?

Come up with strategies together while your child is calm. When he heads into big feeling territory, remind him of his outlets. Come alongside him and comfort him. "I can see this isn't working for you. You're frustrated. Let me help you. Would you like to jump on the trampoline?" When your child has concrete ideas for how he can handle his hard feelings, oh my, he'll be so grateful. When they're coached this way and given real strategies, they come to realize that they can make wise choices no matter how they feel.

After the upset has passed and your child feels better, point this out to him. Feelings come and go — both positive and negative feelings. Little children sometimes feel trapped by their overwhelming feelings. Remind them that they can have difficult feelings, move through them, emerge on the other side, and they'll be okay. Not only okay, but stronger and wiser.

CHAPTER FIVE

Empathy

If your emotional abilities aren't in hand, if you don't have self-awareness, if you are not able to handle your distressing emotions, if you can't have empathy and have effective relationships, then no matter how smart you are, you aren't going to get very far.

DANIEL GOLEMAN

I attended some very fancy schools full of lots of smart people thinking up big stuff. Coming from a blue-collar background, I found it both exhilarating and terrifying to sit in classrooms with incredibly bright kids, many of whom had been groomed from a young age to take their places among the elite — socially, academically, professionally; whatever mattered most to their parents or to them. I learned during those years, though, that being smart doesn't make you happy, and it won't necessarily lead to success in life. Many talented people shrivel up when they leave school and have to deal with real people, real dirt, real pain. Being smart doesn't mean you understand yourself or how to treat others. It doesn't mean you know how to survive disappointment or how to act like a basically decent human being.

These experiences stayed with me and helped me sift through some of the dominant messages to parents about what our kids need in order to be "successful." Of course I want my children to receive a superb education, and I want them to be prepared to succeed in their chosen vocations, but I know that it's equally (and perhaps more) important that they learn how to deal with setbacks and interpersonal conflict. I know it's *most* important that they grow to be faith-filled persons, capable of sustaining healthy, loving relationships.

In this chapter I want to focus on the gift of empathy. It's important that we put as much emphasis on extending to our children lessons in compassion and kindness as we do in algebra and Mozart. Lessons of the heart are learned primarily through relationships, particularly our first relationships in the family.

Empathy and Community

Scientists, particularly those in the neurosciences, used to examine humans as independent, autonomous little units, but now they are discovering how we're really born for community.[1] We don't experience the world inside a vacuum, randomly bumping into people who are having their own private experiences. We are driven to connection, to companionship, to community. This is how God wired us. Our need for human friendship and fraternity is rooted in the human longing for communion with God. The *Catechism of the Catholic Church* explains that human society "is a requirement of [our] nature. Through exchange with others, mutual service, and dialogue with others, we can develop our potential" (1879).

We actually need relationships and community to feel a sense of peace, to develop a healthy stress system, and to learn how to moderate our emotions. Empathy helps this happen. Empathy allows us to experience social connection, drawing us to one another in moments of celebration and grief: "Empathy — fully expressed in a community of nurturing interdependent people — promotes health, creativity, intelligence, and productivity."[2] According to the scientific literature, empathy involves two distinguishable psychological processes — one emotional and one cognitive. First, empathy is the human ability to tune in to the emotional experiences of another person — to experience what they are experiencing or at least imagine it on some level. This is empathic concern. You're watching a movie and the heroine cries, and you find yourself crying too; your best friend loses her father to cancer, and you can't sleep imagining her grief. We experience sadness, distress, or anxiety in response to the losses or pain of another person, real or fictional. Very young children, even toddlers, can experience empathic concern.

Second, empathy is our cognitive ability to see things from another person's point of view, even if we don't agree with them. This is perspective taking. If you and your spouse have plans to go out for dinner tonight, you ask (I hope) what he or she might want to eat — even if you mention that Mexican sounds good to you. You share your own preference, but you recognize that your spouse might not be in the mood for a zesty burrito. This isn't only good manners; it shows that you can see things from your spouse's point of view. You may notice signs of perspective-taking even in preschoolers. Sometimes your preschooler will sweetly pat his baby sister on the back when she's crying. At other times he might throw a block at the baby and tell her to shut up. This is to be expected! Social development is very complex, but if all goes well, by the time his prefrontal cortex is more developed in the teen years, his capacity for perspective-taking will become quite sophisticated.

Empathy and Self-Knowledge

When I first encountered the scientific research on empathy, I couldn't help but recall Saint Edith Stein's writings on consciousness, empathy, and community. It's an overlooked aspect of her work, which is unfortunate because she was ahead of her time. She saw through a philosophical lens what neuroscience would confirm decades later about the human mind. Early in her philosophical training, Stein was curious about how we humans perceive ourselves in relation to others, and how our yearning for connection is thwarted when we fail to comprehend the experiences of those around us. You never really know somebody until you know her heart: what she cares about, what motivates her, what she fears. Stein believed empathy forms the basis of all social relationships, and that real community, solidarity, and unity are possible only through an "empathic embrace" of the other.[3]

Empathy is a gift that allows us to transcend our own personal drama while we gaze on the beauty in the face or mind of another person. Stein saw that without this capacity for a deep, knowing companionship, we are "locked in a prison of individuality" in which we "take the self as the standard."[4] This is truly a prison, Stein explained, because empathy not only leads you to knowledge of the *other*, it also leads you to greater knowledge of *yourself*.[5]

Did you catch that? I think this insight is breathtaking and adds so much to scientific discussions about how we are made for connection. God made us so that we can only experience true self-knowledge and fulfillment in the context of authentic, loving relationships.[6] I think in many ways true empathy is a form of contemplation. When we are absorbed by the reality of another person — their pain, joy, suffering, beauty, or even just the joke they're telling — we're surrendering ourselves and our self-consciousness, even if imperfectly. Paradoxically, only in self-surrender can we come to know who we really are beneath our armor of self-consciousness.

The family is the greatest school of empathy and the first place our children will practice this empathic contemplation. Stein, in particular, believed that the "hidden oneness" experienced within small, intimate communities like the family is necessary to prepare us for a more encompassing connection to society, and eventually to humanity and God himself. We parents recognize this hidden oneness in our families: Even though each of us is so very different — with unique talents, struggles, personalities, and appearances — we experience a quiet knowing that makes us, well, an *us*. When Catholic parents cooperate with God to build and protect this sense of communal identity in their homes, God can sow seeds of trust, compassion, and empathy in the society their children will eventually build.

Why Empathy Is Endangered

Although humans possess an extraordinary and unique potential for empathy, it's only a potential. It has to be nourished and cultivated or it lies dormant. And we are all the worse for it. People who lack empathy have overwhelming difficulties in interpersonal relationships. They have difficulty trusting others, and they reveal little of themselves to anyone. They may perceive our feelings as hostile when we aren't even angry. They may ignore us when we are hurt or sad, because they don't recognize the subtleties of human emotion in other people. They may misinterpret us and our intentions, because they interpret things we say from their own perspectives, and not ours. But do we really need to worry about this with our own children? Given the emphasis in recent decades on social tolerance and antibullying in our schools, we'd expect empathy to be at an all-time high. Aren't we living in the most caring country in the world, in the most caring period of history? Maybe not.

If recent scientific research is accurate, kids are becoming less empathic than previous generations. In one study that looked at freshman college students over more than thirty years,[7] the students were asked to agree or disagree with statements such as, "I sometimes try to understand my friends better by imagining how things look from their perspective" and "I often have tender, concerned feelings for people less fortunate than me." The empathy rating dropped the most sharply in kids entering college after the year 2000, and it has continued to drop. Not surprisingly, the students' narcissism ratings increased while their empathy scores decreased. A leading analyst commented that these kids are called "Generation Me" because they are "the most self-centered, narcissistic, competitive, confident, and individualistic [group] in recent history."[8]

I don't want to jump on the "kids these days" bandwagon. Every generation seems to complain about some deficit in the generation that follows their own. Surely there are many wonderful youths with caring hearts. I teach writing and literature to homeschooled high schoolers, and many of them are passionate about social issues and the plight of the poor; they really want to make a difference. But it's admittedly troubling that an increasing number of college freshmen would admit that they never really think about the perspectives of their friends or give much thought to the needy in their midst. What's going on?

Social Media and the Illusion of Closeness

There are many potential factors contributing to this problem of a lack of empathy. Social media is likely one of them. We shouldn't be surprised that many young people remain self-centered as they enter adulthood when their "relationships" are pursued mostly online. Their often obsessive quest for superficial, even illusory, forms of closeness is destroying our children's appetite for emotional and psychological intimacy — the most complex levels of attachment in the six-stage attachment model that I discussed in chapter 1. As I explain below, the "social brain" needs practice to grow, and that practice comes through real social interactions, not virtual ones.

Even when teenagers or young adults gather together in person (you know, for an actual human conversation), they often have a hard time tuning in to one another. One of them is nearly always checking his or her phone at some point. True sharing and self-revelation are impossible when you expect others to check out regularly, or when you're only superficially invested in the conversation. This is an issue all modern parents should contemplate as we set rules for technology use, especially when our kids are with us or their friends.[9] Of course, the question is: Are they disconnected emotionally because of technology, or are they searching for comfort in technology because they're emotionally disconnected? Whatever the case may be, we want to nourish our children's appetite for real, healthy relationships.

Peer Orientation and the Flight from Vulnerability

Another explanation for the decline in empathy in teens and young adults is peer orientation, an issue introduced in the last chapter. Peer orientation happens when children emotionally orbit around each other rather than their parents and the adults responsible for their wellbeing.[10] If your child is attached to a friend, that's not a problem. The problem arises when you as the parent are replaced by your child's friend as his *primary* attachment figure. Your child can't depend on another child to get his emotional needs met.

One of the extraordinary things about human beings is our emotional vulnerability. We are easily wounded. Yet it's only by taking emotional risks that we can open ourselves up to deep connection and caring. As Dr. Deborah MacNamara puts it, "we cannot experience euphoric states like love and joy without running the risk of experiencing despair and loss. Love is the doorway through which feelings of loss open up. Feelings of despair come in the wake of losing something we care about deeply."[11]

Before we can feel full, we have to be capable of feeling empty; we can't feel the fulfillment of love if we can't also say, "I miss you." In healthy children, their hearts remain soft and vulnerable even in the face of loss, disconnection, or even wounding from their peers because they are shielded by their secure attachment to their parents. The more a securely attached child feels she matters to her parents, the less she cares what her peers think of her. Signs of vulnerability are often shamed by peers, but the securely attached child cares less what the peers think of her than what her parents think of her. She can take a chance at being hurt, because her heart has a secure home base in her parents.

Not so for peer-oriented children. Without the shield of parental connection, it's too risky to move about in the world with a soft heart. They have no emotional home base, so they can't risk being vulnerable. They understand intuitively that it's not safe to be vulnerable with other kids. Without a safe adult to turn to, and under too much threat from peer wounding, a child's brain shuts down her ability to feel vulnerable emotions like missing and caring. The brain can't reduce the wounding children heap on one another, but it can reduce how much they feel the wounds.[12] The child will no longer say things like "I miss you" or "he hurt my feelings," because she won't care. It's a defense mechanism that helps her survive, but at great cost. One of those costs: The caring part of the brain doesn't get what it needs to develop, to a greater or lesser degree, depending on the strength or weakness of the child's bond to her parents.

Just to be clear, *all* kids naturally build up an emotional defense to protect themselves in challenging or hurtful circumstances. When they're at school where people are bugging them or even just evaluating them, their defenses go up. They become a little alarmed, so their brains protect them by numbing them out, so to speak. Their brains preserve basic functioning so they can focus in algebra class and eat their lunches. The same thing happens to adults. Anytime I have to do public speaking, my alarm increases and my brain numbs me out so I can survive! But then we all return to our secure bases — children to their adults, me to my husband — and we're able to let down our guard and our soft feelings come back. Sometimes we vent or complain about our ordeals, then we return to an emotional equilibrium and the defenses come down. This is natural and healthy. As long as we have a release and the softness returns, the defenses aren't a problem.

The problem is that in peer-oriented kids, the defenses become stuck, and their hearts harden. Hardness and callousness is becoming an affect that teenagers try on for size, because they think it's somehow admirable and grown-up. This is not something we want our kids to emulate. I think when many kids walk around with those hardened exteriors, it's just an act. They're trying to survive in their often vicious social environments (also known as high school). But in his many years of work with at-risk youth, Gordon Neufeld was astonished to discover that in the most peer-oriented kids (usually bullies and sometimes sociopaths), their coldness and lack of concern for others wasn't an act; they really didn't care about the pain or suffering of others. They couldn't care less about perspective-taking and community-building.

The more peer-oriented a child, the less empathic she is, period. You can set up empathy classes or antibullying campaigns at schools, but if the students are peer-oriented, it will have little impact on the way they understand and treat each other. The answer to the lack of empathy in peer relationships is not dumping more money into school programs; it's encouraging the strength of the parent-child bond.

Peer Orientation, Social Media, and Discipleship

The social media avalanche has created a widening chasm between believers and the unevangelized because of the often caustic, divisive tone that erupts when somebody disagrees with your opinion. (It's even more shameful when Catholics do this to each other! Do we realize what's at stake?) It's easy to be nasty when you can't see the eyes of the person on the other end of the post. Sherry Weddell in *Forming Intentional Disciples* remarks, "Each generation is largely responsible for the evangelization of its own. But trust cannot be built if the evangelizers regard the unevangelized with fear and disdain."[13] So true, and a lack of empathy is one of the causes of this fear and disdain.

Disciples also need the kind of vulnerability that peer-oriented kids avoid. Christ warned his followers that only those with a docile, teachable heart, only those willing to accept hard truths, would be capable of the long road of discipleship. To take the first step on that road, our children have to be teachable and open to receiving our traditions and values. After that first step, as their faith and commitment to Christ matures, they'll need the courage to step out on their own two feet and proclaim the truth, even when it's unpopular. This is what disciples do. A disciple is capable of perspective-taking and compassion in dialogue with the lost. This gets the conversation started. But disciples are never willing to compromise the truth in their evangelization. They don't "go along to get along."

Peer-oriented kids struggle to be themselves; they resist saying or doing anything unpopular; they aren't interested in the viewpoints or the salvation of anybody. Some peer-oriented kids can take the first step on the path of discipleship. Maybe some cute Christian girl or guy will invite them to join a youth Bible study; if so, they'll go for the peer connections and the support they get from these groups. But peer-oriented kids will never risk anything for the sake of Christ or the salvation of souls. They won't survive the long road. Christ always knew that he would lose some followers because they would ultimately reject challenging truths or because their hardness of heart would lead them astray (see Jn 6:64).

Raising an Empathic Child

Small children are by nature egocentric. It's not their fault; it's just the way little people come to us. But I hope you're as convinced as I am that God doesn't mean for them to stay that way. As the directors of our children's spiritual lives, we can offer many experiences that cultivate empathy as they mature. I'll boil them down to these three areas of practice:

1. Nurture the caring brain.
2. Model empathy.
3. Be an emotion coach.

Nurture the Caring Brain

In chapter 1, I described the dynamic of attachment in childhood. Through repeated interactions with their parents, children develop an internal working model for all their relationships: They learn what to expect in relationships, how much they can trust others, and how safe it is to express their feelings. It turns out, when you choose to live with your child in a way that protects and builds his secure attachment to you, you're also building his caring brain.[14] Securely attached children have better-functioning corpus callosums — the band of nerve tissue running down the middle of the brain which helps the two sides of the brain "communicate" back and forth. Because the left and right hemispheres of the brain are linked up better in emotionally secure children, they can pick up on emotional cues in others (right-brain strength) and find the words for understanding those feelings (left-brain strength) far more easily than insecurely attached children.[15] Their "caring brain" just gets more exercise than less secure kids. Securely attached kids literally build more gray matter in the caring parts of the brain. Secure attachment not only protects your child's emotional health, but it readies his heart for the empathic embrace of others in their full and complicated humanity.

Fill the Attachment Cup to Overflowing

To nurture your child's caring brain, strengthen and deepen the roots of his attachment to you, especially in the early years. Focus on the six phases of developmental attachment:

proximity, sameness, belonging, significance, love, and being known. These are six different ways you can deepen your connection with your child while he builds that caring brain. Fill his tank up in these six ways. In fact, fill it to overflowing. Why overflowing? Why not "just enough"? Because it's only when a child's relational needs are satiated that he will be at peace, so that he can get on with the task of growing his caring brain.[16]

The care we provide must be greater than our children's pursuit of attachment. We don't want our children to be preoccupied with whether they matter to us or whether we might disappoint or scare them today. They need to be able to take our love for granted so they are at rest emotionally. So we offer them more proximity, sameness, belonging, significance, love, and being known than their tank can possibly hold. To quote Luke 6:38, we want to give them these gifts in "good measure, pressed down, shaken together, [and] running over."

In chapter 1, I talked about the attunement between a securely attached child and her parent. Sensitive parents are very good at reading their child's cues about what she needs, and, over time, the child becomes increasingly better at communicating his needs. However, we shouldn't make the mistake of meeting a child's needs only when we see the cuess. We shouldn't let the child take the lead in the dance of attachment. We must take the lead. When we're too passive and always wait for a child to express his needs, the attachment roots might establish themselves, but they are shallower. We can get in front of the needs and meet them before the child starts expressing them. So instead of waiting for a child to ask for a hug, we offer generous hugs. Instead of waiting for a child to ask us if we love her, we tell her every chance we get. We won't do this perfectly, of course. It's the principle we should keep in mind.

Build an Attachment Village
The reliable love of mom and dad are the primary source for secure attachment in the infant, toddler, and preschool years,

but as our children mature, other adults can form part of their secure base. Grandparents, aunts, and uncles create a natural, expanded attachment village; but as many of us live far away from extended family, we have to work a little harder to find caring adults who will connect with our children. Particularly as a child enters the teen years, we can introduce him to adults who create a network of care as he clarifies his goals and explores his unique identity and mission as a Christian. This village for a teen might include a parish leader, a teacher, or professionals in fields that interest him.

My oldest child, Aidan, had several special grown-ups in his life when he was a teenager. Our parish youth group, Civil Air Patrol, and family friends were a rich source of mentors and role models for him. He developed a particularly important relationship with a teacher, Bob Villareal, or "Mr. V" as his students called him. Mr. V taught Aidan and his three closest friends Greek and Roman literature from the time they were in middle school through to their high school graduation. The boys saw Mr. V every week for many years, which allowed the relationship to grow roots. Aidan tells me now that Mr. V was the first adult other than his parents who took an interest in him and wanted to hear his ideas, opinions, and plans for the future. Through and in between reading Homer, Plutarch, and Sophocles (among others), the four boys learned from a former Marine, extreme climber, and devout Catholic what it takes to be a man of substance. They engaged in political debates, pondered the meaning of life, and ate cake every week. Mr. V not only helped shape Aidan intellectually, but he provided a unique model of valor and fidelity for him as he entered adulthood.

This is the way God meant for our children to grow up: surrounded by loving adults who can shepherd them toward maturity. Through your generous love and the love of all the adults in his attachment village, your child's heart can remain soft and vulnerable.[17] With a soft heart, he can get on with the work of growing up rather than growing his Facebook "likes." With a soft heart, he'll become resilient and confident rather than dependent on his peers for his sense of self-worth. With a soft heart, eventually he'll be capable of the empathic embrace that Saint Edith Stein wrote about. If all goes well, by the grace of God, he'll be able to forget himself while he listens to the stories of struggle and joy that others might have to share, and he'll be able to speak the truth with love even when his peers disagree with him.

Model Empathy

How I treat other people in front of my children models for them how to feel about and treat these people. I am very aware that my interest in and care for my neighbors, fellow parishioners, and the grocery store clerk will make a lasting impression on my kids. They will internalize and mirror my attitudes toward these people. Our family faith should include discussions about how we as Christians are called to serve the weakest among us, not only in our communities, but in our own homes. In our family prayers, we can include petitions for the suffering, the sick, and the needy. This will bring to our children's consciousness that other people have experiences and challenges that are very different from their own.

The most powerful way we can model empathy for a child is to treat her with empathy. Developmental psychologist Alan Sroufe is adamant: "How do you get an empathic child? You get an empathic child not by trying to teach the child and admonish the child to be empathic; you get an empathic child by being empathic with the child. The child's understanding of relationship can only be from the relationships he's experienced."[18] We empathize with our children when we affirm their experiences and fears and express curiosity about their opinions. We empathize by simply putting ourselves in their shoes and trying to see things from their perspective. This can be a challenge, because a child's perspective is so mysterious sometimes. This is especially true with young children. Adults express themselves primarily in words, but young children tend to express themselves through their behavior and play. Adults generalize and make predictions based on past experiences, but young children live entirely in the present and see things very concretely. So, they won't articulate their concerns very clearly when they're young. When my own kids were little, to empathize I'd simply point out what I saw. "Your shoulders seem tense" or "You seem nervous about something; your leg is rocking." I've found that empathizing this way de-escalates many brewing emotional storms. Even though my youngest is now eight and my oldest is twenty, I still take this approach because it's a softer invitation to conversation than asking my kids directly to tell me about their problems.

When we empathize this way, not only are we nourishing that caring brain, but it helps our children feel understood, so they feel safe in sharing their feelings and fears with us. This capacity for vulnerability and self-revelation prepares them for the deepest and most complex stages of attachment: emotional and psychological intimacy, the last two stages in Neufeld's attachment paradigm.

Be an Emotion Coach

In the last chapter on discipline, I talked about the important role of the emotions in human flourishing. The emotions influence our choices either positively or negatively: positively when, for example, anger over an injustice propels us to intercede on behalf of the victim; negatively, for example, when in a blind rage we physically assault another person. The difference between the two is in the integration of the mind and the emotions so they positively impact the will. Through merciful discipline, our children can become more emotionally and morally integrated. Here I'd like to expand on those points. We can nourish a child's capacity for empathy by helping her grow into her emotions rather than fearing them or avoiding them. She can't recognize and respect the feelings of others if she isn't capable of doing that for herself. Though a child's empathy muscles are pretty weak when she's little, with our support and guidance, she can strengthen them. Children generally don't understand their emotions. They don't even know what they are, let alone how to manage them. They know they feel uncomfortable or out of control, but they don't know why. Through emotion coaching, children can gain insights into their own emotional lives. They can learn to identify their emotions and their own emotional triggers, and they can learn healthy ways to deal with emotional overload. With this kind of self-awareness, they can begin to recognize and empathize with the emotions and experiences of other people.

Emotion coaching isn't something that comes naturally to most parents. In his classic book on emotional intelligence, John Gottman describes four categories of parents.[19] First are **dismissing parents** who ignore or trivialize their child's negative emotions ("Stop it, you have nothing to be sad about"). These parents show little interest in trying to understand what the child is saying or feeling. They may try to distract the child to shut down the feeling. They believe on some level that negative emotions are harmful or toxic. Children of dismissing parents come to believe that either their feelings are bad or they as a person must be damaged in some way because of their feelings.

Second, **disapproving parents** are similar to dismissing parents, but they are more harsh and negative. They criticize, judge, and punish the child for expressing her negative feelings even if she isn't misbehaving. They believe the child is using her emotional expression to manipulate them. They might also believe emotions are a sign of weakness. The outcomes for the children of disapproving parents are similar to those of dismissing parents, but emotional wounding will be deeper.

Third are **laissez-faire parents**. These parents can be quite warm and caring, and to their credit, they accept all emotional expressions in a child and comfort her when she's upset. But they are too permissive and fail to set limits on the child's behavior, including how she expresses her emotions. Laissez-faire parents seem to believe that it is enough just to let the child blow off steam. Their kids never learn to understand their feelings or how to express them in socially and morally acceptable ways. Being a warm, caring parent isn't enough to raise emotionally intelligent kids (though it certainly goes a very long way). Unfortunately, many parenting experts advise parents to empathize with their child's feelings and comfort him, but they never explain to these parents how to move forward from there. No wonder these parents are confused.

Finally, Gottman describes **emotion coaching parents**. These parents know what to do beyond comforting a child when he's upset. They tend to be very attuned to the child's moods, noticing when she seems "off." They can tolerate being around angry, sad, or frightened children without becoming impatient. They don't tell the child how she should feel, nor do they feel it's their job to fix all the child's problems for her. Instead, they set limits on emotional expression while helping the child figure out how to solve a problem herself. Children of these parents learn that their feelings are okay and that they are capable of resolving conflicts with others.

Coaching Know-How

Through ordinary family experiences, children can begin to develop habits of empathic contemplation that will continue to deepen in adulthood. Here are three ways you can become an all-star emotion coach.

1. Label Emotions for Your Child

When I first read that parents should label emotions for their children, I thought it sounded corny. "You're feeling sad." "I see you're angry." It seemed very contrived, and I guess in some ways it is. But here's why labeling emotions for young children is so important: A child cannot manage emotions he can't name.[20] Naming the emotion helps the child begin to connect the physical sensation in his body with an emotion. This allows two things to happen. First, he can "use his words" about what he's feeling because, well, he has words! He can describe or explain what he feels rather than lashing out. Second, when a child can name his feelings, eventually he'll be able to reflect on them and have second thoughts about acting out on them. This is the tempering effect of emotional integration: The child has an impulse to act out (maybe to hit his sister), but he has second thoughts (he realizes he loves his sister). He feels both at the same time: his angry feelings (hit) and loving feelings (not hit), and these mixed feelings help him to make a good choice.[21] So building up your child's emotion vocabulary is a step toward self-regulation.

Introduce into your home books and games about feelings. Enjoy reading the books or exploring the games together; then when your child is struggling and needs emotion coaching, you'll be able to communicate with him more easily. For children aged three through seven, I highly recommend *My Moods, My Emotions Flipbook for Kids*, which is a spiral bound book of illustrated cards about emotions. On one side of each card is an emotion, while on the other side are different actions the child can take in response to that emotion. The flipbook has twenty different emotions, including bored, confused, disappointed, embarrassed, and frustrated. My daughter Lydia still uses this flipbook. Sometimes she finds the emotion she's feeling, and then she plants the flipbook on the countertop next to my coffee pot where she knows I'll see it (because I visit that spot so many times during the day). She knows I'll know how she's feeling, especially when it's hard for her to talk about it.

For children ages five and up, I like the Thoughts and Feelings: A Sentence Completion Card Game (Bright Spots Games), which was developed by a play therapist. The cards are conversation starters; you can use the cards alone or in conjunction with any ordinary board game. I read once that many adults can identify only three emotions. Maybe we can learn to name our emotions along with our children! When kids can name their emotions, they can learn strategies for making wise choices even when they're feeling bad. They need concrete ideas for what they can do when they're experiencing an overwhelming emotion. These are coping tools or outlets. When your child is in a good mood (or after he's calmed down following an outburst), brainstorm specific actions he might take when he's feeling sad, mad, bored, and so on. Depending on your child's age and personality, these coping tools will be different. Some kids might like to draw or play the piano; other kids might want to punch a pillow or jump rope. You can even turn it into a project and create a book listing his strategies. Then, when he's beginning to have a big emotion, remind him of his strategies. These strategies are not only practical, but they allow your child to practice several virtues: wisdom, temperance, self-control, flexibility, and prudence.

2. Teach Communication Skills

Kids sometimes have a hard time communicating respectfully when they're anxious or angry. But they can learn. By working through conflicts with us or their siblings, children begin to recognize and consider the needs and feelings of others. Peer friendships are less fruitful for these kinds of lessons. A friend can pick up his ball and go home, but a sibling or parent isn't going anywhere. Our children are forced to confront the tension between what they want or need, and what other people in the family might want or need. This is where communication coaching really helps. Conflicts become an instrument for emotional growth and maturity for kids. Communication coaching involves helping kids (1) speak so others can hear them and (2) listen to what others are saying.

First, when your child speaks rudely or disrespectfully to you or a sibling, gently remind her about your family rules regarding respect and kindness. Explain to her how her mean or loud words make others feel: The other person(s) won't hear her because they feel attacked or scared. Explain that when we tell others what we're feeling or what we need with a respectful tone, they hear us better. Then ask your child to repeat what she said in a more acceptable way. You can give her an example if she needs it.

It's important that our children know we're not dismissing or discounting what they're feeling or saying; we're only asking that they use respectful words. Some kids don't realize how their tone or attitude makes others feel. They don't even think about it; they think only about their own feelings or desires. If we keep our own cool as parents, and explain it to them calmly, they will begin to consider the feelings of others before they speak. When they're little, this awareness takes a very long while to develop, but eventually they'll be able to feel their own hurt while at the same time imagining the hurt of another person and hopefully taking that into account before acting or speaking.

Second, we communication coach when we help our kids listen to the other person in a conflict. Kids (and grown-ups) often talk at rather than with each other when they're upset. If tempers are flaring, first call a cool-off or couch time, until everyone can think straight. Then ask your child what she thinks you or her sibling is trying to say to her. If she doesn't know, you can explain it to her. In sibling conflicts, Dr. Laura Markham reminds parents to be empathetic to both children: Don't take sides, even if you have a sense of who is more "at fault."[22] If one child feels that you're taking the other child's side, he'll feel even more resentful toward the other child and less inclined to consider her feelings.

My two middle children, Claire and Dominic, once got into a squabble while I was out of the house dropping their younger sister off at gymnastics. These two children are only two years apart, and they're best friends. They like to say they're twins. But when they have a conflict, it's often very dramatic. In this case, Dominic put what he thought was a funny picture on Claire's computer screensaver, but Claire didn't like it. She thought it was "gross." (It was apparently a picture of an animal with the head of one of our presidents, but I won't mention what sort of animal or which president.) Dominic began to tease her about the picture, so Claire chased him down the hallway, where she tried to stop him. Dominic resisted, and somehow Claire's knee was hurt in the exchange. At this point, I walked into the house.

Following Markham's advice, I didn't take sides. After they both calmed down, I reminded them of the Cameron-Smith family rules: We are kind; we only roughhouse or engage in practical jokes when all parties are enjoying it; we respect the bodies and belongings of others. I also served as a mediator of perspectives. I tried to get each kid to see the other's viewpoint: Dominic was trying to make Claire laugh, not hurt her; he thought she would like it because their older brother puts funny pictures on both their screensavers. Claire didn't think the picture was funny, and she doesn't like her screensaver changed by anybody. My role was to help them hear each other out, and when necessary, to interpret and clarify for one child what the other was saying.

Most significantly, I didn't fix the problem for them; I gave them tools for solving the problem themselves. My coaching took about five minutes. Fifteen minutes later they were reading a magazine together. Years back, I would have tried to figure out who was more in the right. Often I assumed the older child was more at fault because they should have "known better," or they should have known how to get along with younger siblings. But surely they were not always at fault, and they clearly didn't always know how to get along with their younger siblings. My new approach is much more sensible. There's no way I can be the judge in every conflict, collecting evidence and delivering a fair verdict. When I realized it wasn't doing my kids any good anyway, I was relieved! No more Judge Mom. Communication coaching is in fact easier and my kids are learning valuable relationship skills that they'll bring to other relationships.

It's also important that we remain calm ourselves if we want to teach our children how to communicate with each other. If we freak out when our kids are freaking out, no learning will take place, and the situation will only deteriorate. Sometimes this is easier said than done, but if you can manage to stay calm even 50 percent of the time, you're headed in the right direction. The message we want our kids to receive is "We can get through this" and "Nothing you have is too much for me to handle." We want them to know we are strong enough to hold them up no matter how wobbly they feel. We don't want them to think we are overwhelmed by them (even if we are a little).

3. Teach Problem-Solving Skills

In the discipline chapter, I talked about problem-solving as a discipline tool. Often behavioral issues erupt when a child is facing an overwhelming problem. Sometimes these issues are personal issues having to do with homework, scheduling problems, or frustration about how to complete a task. But sometimes a child is having a conflict with another person — a sibling, friend, or parent — and she doesn't know how to handle it. Often our kids don't need us to help them solve the problem; they just need our calm and supportive physical and emotional presence. At other times, they will ask for our advice about how to approach the conflict, and this is where problem-solving or conflict-resolution skills can help. I'm not suggesting that parents take over and solve all their kids' problems. But I do think offering guidance occasionally is appropriate.

Remind your child of the steps to problem-solving:

- Define the problem and the needs or fears of the people involved.
- Brainstorm solutions to the problem.
- Evaluate the options.
- Pick one.
- Try it.

If the other party in the conflict is a sibling or parent, get all parties involved. Your problem-solving is focused on conflict resolution. As Christians, it's important that our children recognize that in interpersonal conflicts where the two parties are friends or family members, conflict resolution focuses on the interests and well-being of both people. We aren't out to beat the other person at a game; we aren't attempting to pull off a slick business deal. We are trying to serve and care for everyone. This is called principled negotiation. In principled negotiation, we focus on the desire or need of each party and how we can get there in a way that satisfies everyone. Identify and consider each person's need or fear, and search for solutions that will protect all parties. It's a win-win negotiation. In contrast, positional negotiation is cutthroat. You're out to protect your position, so you tend to exaggerate your needs and rights while understating the other person's needs and rights. This is a win-lose, or even a lose-lose, way to negotiate. Positional negotiation is valid in some circumstances (for example, in criminal trials), but not for building healthy relationships.

An example might help. One night after a scouting meeting, Claire and Dominic (yep, the dynamic duo again) were disagreeing about who would sit in the front seat of the car on the drive home. Both kids were presenting reasonable arguments, so I suggested that they go through the conflict-resolution steps. Claire believed that because she's older than Dominic, and because she gets motion sickness in the back seat, she should get the front seat. Dominic believed that because he's taller than Claire, he needs more leg room, so he should get the front seat. In the end, they decided to try a schedule: Claire has dibs on the front seat on Sunday, Monday, and Tuesday, and Dominic has dibs on the other days. But because Claire gets motion sickness particularly on long trips, they agreed she would always get to sit in the front seat if we had to drive on the highway for any reason. They settled on a thirty-day trial of this agreement after which they would evaluate whether they should modify it. I wasn't involved in this negotiating (though I did have to sit in the parking lot waiting for them to work things out). They handled this one on their own. At other times, I have had to remind my kids about Christian charity and generosity, and I have had to help younger kids articulate their points to older kids.

What if I had been in a hurry that night to get home? I would have made a decision about who would get the front seat, with the understanding that I would help them work through the problem later. As John Gottman explains, "Parents need to be in a reasonably undistracted (if not calm) frame of mind to [emotion coach] well. It also helps if children are in a relatively teachable state. Thinking strategically, you want to seize opportunities when your child is most likely to be receptive."[23] Sometimes you won't have time for problem-solving or conflict-resolution exercises, so at those moments, don't attempt it. You'll likely end up frustrated or rushing through it, at which point it will be counterproductive. Or at times a child might be too tired, hungry, or emotionally shut down to hear what you have to say. In those instances, just wait. The right moment will come at another time.

Some of you might be thinking that Dominic and Claire, in a gesture of kindness, should have offered the seat to the other sibling. This miracle does happen on occasion in my home, but it's probably not realistic to expect it to happen all the time. I require kindness, but I also allow room for them to work things out together. I do want my children to be capable of generous, self-giving love, but I also want them to know that it's okay to express their desires and to share their needs with the people they love.

With time and practice, kids can become true diplomats and peacemakers. Often we hear how important it is for our children to be leaders, but it's equally important that they learn to be team players and even followers. Recognizing the value of someone else's plan or idea, learning to negotiate her preferences, or managing her feelings of disappointment or anxiety in the face of conflict are all key to a child's future success and well-being. Most importantly, when our children grow up with the capacity to reach across the table to touch an enemy's hand, to find common ground in conflict, and to find fragments of unity when peace seems impossible, we are participating in the Church's mission of transforming society.

CHAPTER SIX

Radiant Faith

In the tender compassion of our God,
the dawn from on high shall break upon us
to shine on those who dwell in darkness
and in the shadow of death,
and to guide our feet into the way of peace.
FROM THE CANTICLE OF ZECHARIAH, LUKE 1:78–79

After arriving at Mass one day, we had just settled into the pew when my daughter Lydia climbed into my lap, stood up, and shouted, "GOD, WHERE ARE YOU?!" She was about three years old. In her preschool mind, Lydia fully expected to encounter God there. Sometimes we can really learn something from our children, can't we?

I'm a Catholic "revert" (a Catholic who left the Church, but later returned). I'm both a convert and a revert, really: I was brought into the Church by my stepfather when I was twelve, but I'd already left by sixteen. I spent many years wandering through different Protestant and nondenominational churches, searching for a spiritual home. When they all proved dissatisfying in some way, I moved on to explore different religions, particularly Buddhism and Hinduism. By the time I was doing graduate studies in England, my confidence in Christianity had been restored. I believed that "the Christ event" was true — that Christ was more than a wise sage or prophet; he was God incarnate. But I wasn't sure where or whether I wanted to practice Christianity formally. I was certain I would never return to the Catholic Church, which I figured was no place for any earnest seeker of spiritual growth. At the time, I was working on my master's thesis on a text written by an English medieval mystic, Margery Kempe. Although I was a student of medieval literature, instead of approaching the text as a literary work, I chose to read Margery's words through the lens of theology. I researched and read up on the history of Eucharistic theology, because Margery often broke down in tears during the consecration. In the process of my research, I don't think I found anything theologically startling about Margery's book, but I did find my way back to the Church.

In contrast to what I'd been told as a teenager by cheerful and well-meaning (and well-trained) Protestant youth leaders, it turns out the Catholic Church did not invent the idea of transubstantiation in the Middle Ages. Early Christians believed in the Real Presence, and Eucharistic theology from the beginning assumed Christ was physically present in the sacrament — not symbolically or spiritually, but *physically* present.[1] And I came to believe it myself. My spiritual journey ultimately led me back to where it had begun. How could I stay away from the Catholic Mass when Christ was physically there, waiting for me to show up?

I remember vividly the first Mass I attended shortly thereafter at the Blackfriars Priory on St. Giles in Oxford. I was surprised by the familiarity of many things — prayers, gestures, and even smells. Even though I'd been in the Church so briefly during my teen years, it still felt like home. While I stumbled over the prayers, I recognized them; I prayed along with the other parishioners, if only in a whisper at times. The prayers were the same ones I had prayed years ago and miles away in the place I'd been baptized and confirmed, the same prayers offered by generations of Christians before me.

But I'm certain I lacked Lydia's faith — her confidence and surrender — in that moment when she called out for God. Children seem to possess an intuitive sense of God's presence. It's a sensitivity that evades many adults unless we work to recover the simplicity and wonder we once had. That's one of the things I love most about being a mother. My children help me recollect what I once knew.

Understanding the Landscape

If children begin life with such an innate faith in the transcendent, why do so many of them end up losing their faith? If recent studies are correct, between one-third and one-half of our children will leave Catholicism when they reach adulthood.[2] That means of my four children, only a couple of them are statistically likely to remain Catholic. Some young adult Catholics move to non-Catholic churches or non-Christian religions, which is bad enough, but we're also witnessing a concerning increase of young people who think that any form of organized religion is passé. Young adults today are twice as likely to describe themselves as agnostic, atheistic, or religiously unaffiliated than young adults thirty or forty years ago.[3] Unfortunately, at some point, our kids will be confronted by the message that it's morally evolved to be "spiritual but not religious," that they're better off living without the shackles of *doctrine* and *creeds*. In fact, in many college classes our kids attend, these two words are disparaged as musty relics that can be appreciated only by those who are fooled or foolish. Being an atheist is actually cool at most secular schools.

I'm concerned that we may exacerbate the problem when we attempt to approach our children's faith formation in the same way our grandparents did. There was a time when Catholic culture provided the glue that bound people and families to the Church. In the United States a hundred years ago, local

Catholic communities were tightly knit and offered everything a family needed — schools, sport leagues, unions, health care, and even newspapers.[4] These cultural ties have eroded. Today most Catholic families have only a thin connection to their parishes and little sense of a coherent Catholic identity.

Given the broader secularist pressures on our kids and the loss of that deeply layered Catholic community, it's no longer enough to put our kids in weekly catechism classes. So how can we raise children who appreciate the gifts of our traditions and the truth of Church teachings while also protecting their natural delight in the divine? Remember the Catholic principle of the common good: We as parents should exercise patience and discernment as we identify the conditions that make it easier for children to develop to their full potential, especially their spiritual potential.

At the outset of this book, I explained that we can evangelize our children by (1) building and protecting the trust and connection between ourselves and our kids; (2) attending to the emotional well-being of our children; and (3) creating a vibrant, beautiful Catholic home culture. The previous five chapters (on love, balance, play, merciful discipline, and empathy) focused largely on the first and second ways of evangelizing children. By nourishing our connection with our children and protecting their emotional well-being, we are making it easier for them to cross the bridge of discipleship. This chapter is about the third way of evangelizing our children. We can build a radiant Catholic home culture that reveals to our children the rituals, stories, saints, art, and music that have shaped and inspired the thinking, behavior, and aesthetic affections of Catholics for over two thousand years. This is our beloved inheritance, left to us to pass on to our own children.

Before I continue, I want to make it clear that by focusing on how you can build a strong Catholic *home* culture, I am not dismissing or minimizing the significance of the culture in our parishes. But few of us learned how to introduce and incorporate Catholic culture into our family lives. When we make an effort to do this, our children begin to feel an integration between "church life" and "home life"; they feel more comfortable with and connected to their parish communities. What's more, the strength and depth of the faith practices of parishioners at home directly impacts the vitality of parish culture.

Building a Catholic Family Culture

Does culture really matter? I've sometimes heard the comment that so-and-so is only "culturally Catholic," suggesting the person is not a particularly committed Catholic. It's true that culture alone isn't enough to bring us to the summit of mature faith, but without culture, faith won't survive. As Church historian Robert Louis Wilken points out, Christian faith cannot be "sustained for long without the support of a nurturing Christian culture."[5]

Wilken carefully studied the emergence of Christian culture in the early centuries — how it happened and why it was successful against all odds. The early Church didn't simply infiltrate culture; it created a culture. It created distinctive experiences and visible markers that held Christians together and helped outsiders identify them as set apart from the larger culture. Christianity wasn't only a message but also a way of life that sustained and nourished believers through ritual, language, practices, and stories. Wilken describes a distinctively Christian "space, time, and language" that allowed early Christians to remember their history, describe their faith experiences, and become firmly rooted in something greater than themselves that could carry Christ's message to future generations.

Wilken's observations apply to the modern domestic church: A distinctively Catholic home culture can provide for our children some of those lost roots in their Catholic heritage. We can strengthen the faith and Catholic identity of our families by exploring the space, time, and language of Catholic culture in everyday family life. Much as the Church herself emerged and took shape as a culture, renewal within Catholic homes can happen at least partly through culture. It's true that culture isn't everything, but it's a pretty good place to start, especially for families. We don't want our children to know only the message of the Church; we also want them to inherit a way of life that can nourish and sustain their faith. From there, our families, gathered as a community of love, will be able to plant the seeds of a much broader Catholic cultural renewal.

Creating Sacred Space in Our Homes

The early Christians created a tangible, distinctly Christian material culture. They pooled their resources and built Christian catacombs to honor their dead. They lovingly decorated the catacombs with beautiful paintings that told the story of their history, including images of Christ as the gentle shepherd and familiar Biblical stories. These were spaces of remembering — remembering not only their departed loved ones, but also remembering where they as a community had come from. Our homes can have the same power of remembrance. The atmosphere of our homes teaches our children what's important to us, whether we're aware of it or not. At the very least, our homes should look different from those of our non-Catholic neighbors. I'm not recommending you turn your home into a monastery! But a few simple visual reminders of our Catholic heritage and beliefs will kindle much curiosity, comfort, and conversation.

My approach is to create an inviting environment in which my kids naturally engage with our Faith as they go about their day. Inspired by what I learned in Reggio Amelia pedagogy, I "plant" little faith invitations around the house. In every room, there is some sort of sacred art, religious statue, or other religious object. For example, as you enter my home, in our foyer near the front door, a small metal holy water font is affixed to the wall. In the living room, you will find a small statue of Our

Lady of Grace and an old china platter holding several rosaries. I love icons, so you will notice little icons around my home, some purchased, some homemade. Now that my youngest is eight years old, I can put out more fragile items, but when my kids were all small, I avoided anything too priceless or fragile. Most rooms in my house have a small stack of religious books, either on tables or in baskets. I also have book display stands; I select a few books to display depending on the liturgical season. This is a way to invite my children to open a book even when I'm not directly leading them.

In one room we have a family altar. This is really the center of our family faith life, a focal point when we gather for family devotions. The altar is on top of an old chest with drawers where I can store our altar linens and other religious items. At all times, a lace runner, candle, cross, small icon, and thurible (a small censer for burning incense) are arranged on the altar. Depending on the liturgical season, I also place different books, religious statues, or other special items on the altar. For example, every year during Lent we place a paschal candle on our altar. On the Feast of the Sacred Heart, I have a Sacred Heart statue that I take out along with an illustrated prayer to the Sacred Heart. During November, the month of All Souls, our family altar is transformed into an altar of remembrance: We create a gallery of photos of our departed relatives, and we offer up special prayers for them every day.

If you don't have a family altar and you'd like to create one, you'll find tons of ideas for them on the Internet. If you'd like a comprehensive and inspiring resource, I recommend *The Little Oratory* by David Clayton and Leila Marie Lawler. Your children will offer you plenty of creative ideas about what to include on your family altar. When my children were little, they liked to place the many treasures they found out in nature on our altar, and I encouraged this. I occasionally found Lego guys and stuffed animals on the altar, all offered in love, I'm sure!

It's not necessary to spend much money to do this. I found

all my religious statues used at thrift stores and on eBay. Think about what you already have on hand: baptismal candles, missals, rosaries. Explain to your children why you care about these objects and describe the stories behind them. Then begin to build your home culture in a way that appeals to you and fits your budget.

Sacred Art and Music for Kids

These visual reminders of our Faith not only teach our kids about the history and traditions of the Church, but they're authentically beautiful. Beauty is a powerful evangelizer! Popular Catholic writer and social-media evangelist Bishop Robert Barron often says (inspired by Hans Urs von Balthasar) that if you want to win somebody for Christ, don't start with truth or goodness; start with *beauty*.[6] What does he mean by this? You may have heard or read a reference to "the good, the beautiful, and the true," perhaps in a homily. In Balthasar's work,[7] these are three philosophic transcendentals of being. The transcendentals are found in everything God has created; they "transcend" all things because they are characteristics that belong to each and every thing. They form desires or interests within all people; they're part of human nature. As humans, we naturally ask questions about these aspects of being. What is the right thing to do (the good)? What is reality and how can I know it (the true)? Wow, what's THAT (the beautiful)?

In our work of evangelization, start with beauty, says Bishop Barron. He isn't suggesting that truth and morality are unimportant. Without question, they're critical to the process of conversion. However, people are often more open to a message of beauty than they are to intellectual arguments or moral rules. They are more likely to take that first step down the path of conversion when we begin by introducing them to the beauty of our Faith. So, instead of explaining to them the five proofs for God's existence or why abortion is wrong, begin by inviting them to *look*. Look at the great art and cathedrals of our Faith, at their immense and resplendent unity and symbolism. Look at Christ's life, at his integrity and his unfathomable self-giving love. Look at the inexplicable and heroic acts of love displayed by the saints. No lectures, no lists to memorize, just something splendid and radiant to gaze upon.

When a person is drawn to the Church's beauty, this can awaken wonder in them about Christianity. Then they will naturally begin to conform their lives to Christ's mission (this is practicing the good), and through living out that mission, they will really begin to understand him (this is grasping the true). You see, beauty can lead others to the good and the true.

Of course, the truth of the Faith can lead us to the good and the beautiful too. I've already mentioned that one of the things that drew me back to the Church was the truth I discovered when I started earnestly reading what she actually teaches. But what sustained my faith as a young, curious Catholic was the beauty of our Faith. Do you know what a gift we have? Not only in our grand treasures, like the Sacré-Coeur basilica in Paris, with its triple bronze doors and magnificent carved stalls, but also in the humble grottos and crumbling abbeys that are bones of majesty and suffering. I could never in my lifetime plumb the depths of what there is to know about the liturgy, art, music, and history of our Church. It's astonishing. The truth led me to the Church's door, but it was beauty that invited me to come in and stay awhile. This is what Bishop Barron is talking about.

How does all this relate to raising children? Well, kids are very responsive and sensitive to the beautiful, especially the beauty found in the created world and the arts. Their aesthetic awareness is engaged very early, but their logical and moral reasoning develops later and more slowly. I think we should keep this in mind when we're creating our family faith culture. Of course, we'll attend to the good and the true in our parenting; we're responsible for giving our children a sound education in the doctrines of the Church and teaching them right from wrong. But it's easy to overlook the necessity of beauty in our children's spiritual lives, as if it's not as important as giving our kids the right information and the right moral code. The good, the beautiful, and the true are really inseparable. When you leave one of them out, it diminishes the clarity of the other two.

So we can nourish and celebrate our children's fascination with beauty. In addition to the ideas offered above, which are appropriate for children of any age, we can begin introducing them to great Catholic art and music as early as preschool. Find a simple coffee-table book displaying images of sacred art, particularly from the medieval period, or simply put on a recording of a great Catholic composer like Palestrina while your children draw or work on a puzzle together. My family enjoys the music released by the Benedictine Sisters of Mary Queen of Apostles. The sisters have music for all the liturgical seasons, including Lent, Easter, Advent, and Christmas.

Since the fourth century, when Christians were finally permitted to worship legally (thanks to Constantine and the Edict of Milan), the Church has been the unparalleled patron of the visual arts, including paintings, mosaics, iconography, metalwork, illuminated manuscripts, and even jewelry. It's never too early to introduce your children to these works of art. I allow my children to look through my graduate school books containing examples of medieval books of hours and other illuminated manuscripts that were created in Catholic monasteries.

Our family recently received the stunning book *The Vatican: All the Paintings* by Anja Grebe, which includes images of the collections in the Vatican Museums — not only the paintings, but many tapestries, illuminated manuscripts, and sculptures. This is one of the books I like to "plant" for my children to explore. It comes with a DVD containing the entire collection, so I can choose some of the images to project onto our television on occasion. It's not as good as visiting in person, but it's a lovely addition to our home library. For families with kids eight years and older, I also recommend Bishop Barron's breathtaking ten-part documentary *Catholicism*, which takes viewers to fifty locations in sixteen different countries to visit the artistic and spiritual treasures of the Church. It's perfect for family movie night!

My purpose with all this isn't to give my kids a college education in art or music history. I just want them to experience real paintings and cathedrals and listen to real music from our religious tradition.[8] Of course, I have children's books and children's music in my home too, but I think every parent can also confidently introduce their kids to the richness found in the great masters. Even if they don't understand what they are seeing or hearing, children develop a taste and affinity for it. This is the big point, really. Even adults don't fully comprehend the truly beautiful. It's subtle, complex, and mysterious. It's something we want to live with and savor, even if we don't completely understand it. Wow, what is that? That is transcendent beauty stirring in us. It is part of what makes life delicious.

So even if you don't know much about these subjects yourself, just expose your children to them. Just show them. The beautiful has a way of working on our hearts even when we don't have words to explain what's happening to us. Being awakened to a thing of beauty isn't like being zapped with a stun gun. If you show your four-year-old an image of Giotto's *Sermon to the Birds*, he won't look up at you and blurt out a ten-point argument for God's omnipresence. Beauty doesn't work like that. Beauty catches our attention and often delights us, drawing our hearts away from less beautiful things.

An encounter with real beauty — especially one that surprises them — can awaken in our children a "nameless yearning for something more than earth can offer. Elegant splendor reawakens our spirit's aching need for the infinite, a hunger for more than matter can provide."[9] Recall the story from chapter

3 about C. S. Lewis playing in his garden as a child, when a sense of joy overcame him, a joy that led him eventually to belief. Perhaps like Lewis, the beautiful art and music (and other Catholic treasures) they experience will deepen our children's natural sense of wonder, and that wonder will point them toward the great vastness of Ultimate Beauty, God himself.

Observing Sacred Time in Our Homes
In addition to sacred space, early Christians created a distinctive culture through time, namely the creation of the Christian calendar. In the chapter on balance, I described how children thrive on regular routines and rhythms; it gives them a sense of peace and security. When I identified a balance problem in my own family, I began making an effort to keep to a regular weekly routine as much as possible. From there, I began introducing family traditions into our year to provide even more rhythm to our lives. Our new traditions were initially tied to the natural seasons: apple-picking in the fall, candle-making in the winter, gardening in the spring. We still do these seasonal activities as a way to anchor our family life throughout the year. But it hit me one day that *hey, we're Catholic — we have rhythm!*

The life of the Church unfolds around the same patterns and rhythms every year: We celebrate the great seasons of Advent and Lent, feast days, and Sunday Mass and holy days of obligation. On top of that, did you know the Church dedicates each month to a particular devotional practice? For example, February is dedicated to the Holy Family and June is dedicated to the Sacred Heart of Jesus. This liturgical rhythm has long ordered and inspired the behavior and affections of Catholics; it's a rich part of our culture. Wilken explains:

> The liturgical calendar makes religious remembrance habitual and familiar. The repetition of saints' days and festivals of the Lord is a kind of spiritual metro-

nome helping communal life to move in concord with the mysteries of the faith. We should not underestimate the cultural significance of the calendar and its indispensability for a mature spiritual life. Religious rituals carry a resonance of human feeling accumulated over the centuries.[10]

Yes, accumulated over the centuries! Incorporating this liturgical metronome into our homes is not only healthy for our children emotionally and spiritually, but it binds us together in Christian communion with centuries (actually millennia) of Christians.

In my own home, celebrating the liturgical calendar breathed real life into our family faith. I was already teaching my kids the basics of the Faith and reading Bible stories with them, but something special happened when we began adding celebrations of the Church year to our family routines and seasonal plans. When you have small children, these practices are downright fun. We added a Jesse Tree at Advent, a little moss-covered crucifixion scene in the base of a planter during Lent, and family tea parties on saints' days. We began inviting other friends to our celebrations. We've hosted multifamily gatherings in October to pray the Rosary in honor of the Month of the Most Holy Rosary. I make a giant rosary out of cupcakes and candles!

Catholic families can also celebrate personal religious days. Some families I know celebrate the anniversary of their child's baptism or First Holy Communion. On my children's name days (the feast day of the saint who shares their birth name), we have celebrations that reflect the child's patron saint. For example, on the Feast of Saint Dominic, the patron saint of astronomers, we go stargazing because of the legend that a star settled on Saint Dominic's brow when he was baptized. Saint Lydia was a maker of purple cloth, so on Lydia's name day we have tried several tie-dying projects and making natural dye out of berries.

Don't fear: These playful ways of engaging our children's imaginations won't diminish the dignity of the Faith. Not only is it the perfect way to introduce the beautiful aspects of our Faith that I described above (sacred art and music), but young children in particular benefit from a playful, tangible approach to faith formation. As Mary Reed Newland puts it, "We learn to swim in the shallow water before we are able to swim in the deep. These delightful things to see and touch and smell and taste and hear and make and do are by far the best tools there are to teach of the beauty and power of God, and the richness of life in Christ."[11] Children experience the world through their senses. Engaging their imaginations with fun, hands-on experiences of Jesus and the whole story of salvation prepares their hearts and minds for deeper doctrinal and theological messages. The Church calendar is part of our Catholic identity: Why not make it delightful, delicious, and beautiful?

And I have to tell you something. Living the Church year in creative ways with my children has deepened my own faith too. As I return with my children to the same prayers, stories, and images each year, they don't remain the same for me. I respond anew with deeper understanding and greater fondness. The liturgical calendar is filled with a gentle and sure rhythm of grace, special signs to me from God of his love and protection. As I point my children toward Christ, I find him more myself.

Introducing Children to Real Heroes

I think kids will always have heroes. In their littleness, they look for somebody extraordinary to look up to, somebody they can aspire to follow in some way as they grow up. By reading, watching, and thinking about the lives of their heroes, kids are able to envision themselves differently. They can imagine a path to becoming more excellent like their heroes. For some reason, though, just being athletic, powerful, good-looking, or

famous is enough to make somebody a hero nowadays. Some
of today's most popular "heroes" are not worth our kids' time.
It's okay for our kids to admire people who possess a special talent or skill, but we can teach them that there's a difference between talent and heroism. We can teach them that
heroism is correctly measured by a person's character and holiness, not his bank account or batting score. We can begin
by introducing them to the saints. Not only are the saints "a
Catholic thing," but the saints are true heroes who possessed
uncommon virtue; they placed their faith above all things. We
want our kids to get to know these heroes as well as they know
the winner of *America's Got Talent*.

From a young age, read stories about the saints to your
kids, watch movies about them, and celebrate their feast days
in your home. When your kids are little, these stories will form
images and narratives that will become life lessons for them as
they mature. Older children who grew up with favorite saints
tend to transition easily to more sophisticated hagiography
that contains greater details about the struggles and sacrifices
of these saints, and their often enigmatic courage and generosity even in the face of cruelty.

Teenagers are especially hungry for heroes. They are looking for somebody to pattern their lives after. Hopefully they encounter the saints when they're little so that their attraction to
particular saints unfolds naturally as they mature. When they
realize that the saints were real people, not mythical characters in a story, they can be deeply impacted. They're old enough
to understand that their favorite saints were born as ordinary,
imperfect people who sought and developed virtue because of
a burning desire to increase in friendship with Christ. Some of
the saints had really disreputable beginnings, but as they grew
in virtue, they thirsted more for union with God, and they were
transformed increasingly into the image of Christ himself.

When he was a teenager, my son Aidan was interested
in the life of Saint Maximillian Kolbe, a Franciscan friar and

priest who sheltered many refugees during World War II, including two thousand Jews fleeing Nazi persecution. Eventually he was arrested and sent to Auschwitz. When several men were selected to die by starvation, Kolbe wasn't one of the men chosen, but he volunteered to take the place of another man who was a father. This act of sacrificial love and unflinching courage was a divine-like gesture. Earlier I talked about aesthetic beauty — the visual and musical gifts of our Catholic heritage. Kolbe is an example of the beautiful gesture — a single act that breaks open in front of our eyes with radiant, transcendent meaning. He sacrificed his life for a stranger. Here is the beautiful gesture, pointing our gaze toward Christ whose Great Gesture opened the gates of heaven for us.

These are the sort of heroes we want our children to admire and emulate. Of course, many heroes aren't canonized saints. Think of great historical figures like Moses, Abraham Lincoln, and Martin Luther King Jr. And don't forget the heroes living among us (priests, teachers, aunts, uncles) who possess a special gift, talent, or passion and choose to use it to help others or to meet a need in some way. They place God first, they trust in God's promises, and they strive to love as Christ loves. These are all great heroes who deserve our children's attention.

Family Prayer Habits

Family prayer is a great way to model for children how to look to God for all that is good and to express gratitude for our blessings and sorrow for our failings. Many families pray together before meals and at bedtime, which is a great place to start. I'd like to offer you some more ideas for enriching your prayer life together.

The Divine Office

Not only do we have the liturgical calendar to provide rhythm to our faith lives, but we have a daily rhythm of prayer available in the Liturgy of the Hours, also called the Divine Office or the Breviary. The Liturgy of the Hours is an ancient form of prayer which includes a series of psalms, Scripture readings, and prayer intentions. Priests and vowed religious are required to pray the Hours, and the laity are encouraged to pray it too, as a way to join with the universal Church in offering to God our daily work, play, and rest.

If you're really motivated, the Hours can be used for prayer every three hours (morning, midmorning, midday, midafternoon, evening, and before bed), but few families can keep this schedule given the limits of our time and our children's attention spans. Even active religious are given permission to adapt the schedule to their ministry, so it's perfectly fine to adapt the prayers to your family's schedule and needs. What you do should come from a desire to grow closer to God and to each other, not from a sense of obligation or guilt. Also consider the age of your children. I didn't start praying the Hours with my kids until my youngest was over five, but I know other families who start earlier. Whatever works for your family is fine.

Most families who want to try the Hours at home pick one or two of the major hours (usually morning, noon, or evening) and use those prayers for regular family devotions. In my home, I skip over some of the prayers (for example, I pick one of the psalms) so that my younger kids don't become distracted. I want to be forthright: The Hours can be intimidating when you first look at them. There's a four-volume set, but most laity use the condensed, one-volume *Christian Prayer*.[12] Even this condensed version is a fat book (two thousand pages) and requires some flipping around to different sections. Some folks feel discouraged from starting or continuing the practice because they can't figure out what they're supposed to do or where they should be in the book every day. You can buy a separate small guide (it's only a few dollars), released annually, which tells you exactly which pages you should use each day of the year.

We have *Christian Prayer* (the fat book), but in my home we mostly use *Shorter Christian Prayer*,[13] which is published by the same company. *Shorter Christian Prayer* includes only the morning, evening, and night prayers, and a selection of prayers for the seasons and feast days. It's much more manageable and easier to understand than the fat book. It's also much more affordable, so depending on your budget, you can give all your older children their own *Shorter Christian Prayer* to use during family prayer. One year at the beginning of Lent, I gave all my children their own copy. They felt very grown up. Once you use this shorter breviary for a few weeks, you will figure it out. The effort is more than worth it. I find the psalms come to mind when I need them, and I know these beautiful prayers are working in my children's souls too.

You can also find an app for the Liturgy of the Hours.[14] Using the book teaches you how the different parts of the Hours work together, so if you do eventually use the app, it will make more sense. On the other hand, maybe the app will help you get started, and using the app while traveling is definitely convenient. Do what works best for your family.

Lectio Divina

In my home, we use the Liturgy of the Hours for family prayer at certain times of the year. At other times, I lead my children in *Lectio Divina* (sacred reading). *Lectio Divina* is an old monastic form of meditation on a passage from Sacred Scripture. This prayer practice is easy to use at home, and you can find resources specifically for use with kids.[15]

Briefly, the steps in *Lectio Divina* are:

1. *Lectio* (**reading**): Read aloud to your children a text from Sacred Scripture, usually from the daily Mass readings. At this stage, we are just reading it and understanding it as the Church teaches it; we aren't applying it to our own lives yet. Sometimes

at this stage I explain the historical context of the passage to my kids, if I have that background.

2. *Meditatio* (**meditation**): Have your children close their eyes, then read the text aloud again very slowly. Before you read it, tell your children to imagine themselves in the scene or to think about how the passage applies to them or to a situation they're thinking about. What comes to mind? Does a particular word or phrase stand out to them?

3. *Oratio* (**prayer**): Next we pray together. We speak freely with God in our own words, thinking about the passage. We may be inspired to ask for the intercession of a particular saint. We can offer petitions, offer thanks, and praise God.

4. *Contemplatio* (**contemplation**): Sit quietly for two to five minutes, depending on the ages of your kids. Ask them to keep these questions in mind: What is God's will for me? Am I concerned about a particular problem? What is God saying to me about this problem? How is God calling me today in particular?

A *Lectio* resource will guide you through these steps. If you want to pray the *Lectio* alone before you start a practice with your whole family, the Carmelites have a free online daily guided *Lectio* for adults (www.ocarm.org). I use it several times a week. You can also read their background information on a Scripture passage to prepare for *Lectio* with your kids, in case they have questions!

The Rosary

The Rosary is probably the quintessential Catholic devotion, and it's easy for kids to pray, including really young children. Ideally, each child should have his own rosary. You can find rosaries with large beads made especially for toddlers. I once made my friend's child a Rosary play mat: I appliquéd a rosary onto the mat, and made separate felt rosettes for the child to hold and place on each appliqué "bead" while her family prayed. I think the rosettes ended up being used as projectiles, but it was a fun idea!

May is the Month of the Blessed Virgin Mary, and October is the Month of the Holy Rosary, so in those months our family devotions center on the Rosary. When my children were all young, we usually prayed only one decade along with reading reflections and offering personal prayers. I like to have images for my children to meditate on while we pray. I like books with sacred art representing the mysteries, such as *The Rosary in Art for Children* by Mary Clooney or *The Sacred Art Rosary Flipbook* by William Bloomfield, but any book with large illustrations will do.

The Stations of the Cross

During Lent, my family prays the Stations of the Cross together every Friday. One parish close to us has an outdoor Stations of the Cross. I take a book to guide us while we walk and pray the Stations together. If we can't get to that parish, we pray the Stations at home using just the book. For this reason, I like to find books with beautiful illustrations of the Stations. If all your children are small, I recommend *The Story of the Cross* by Mary Joslin or *Stations of the Cross for Children* by Julianne Will. Both these resources provide a simple but engaging introduction to the Stations for young kids. If you have a wide age range in your home as I do, my favorite resource is *Mary's Way of the Cross* by Richard Furey. This resource was so affordable (a few dollars) that I was able to buy all my children their own copies. If your kids are all older than ten, I love Caryll Houselander's *The Way of the Cross*.

You can also create Stations in your home using large Stations cards taped up in a hallway, which you can find on most Catholic gift and supplies websites. My friend Marcia and her husband created a rustic hiking Stations of the Cross on her farm. It's breathtaking! I dream of adapting it to my suburban back garden someday.

Why should we try the Divine Office, *Lectio Divina*, or the Rosary? It gets our family into a habit of praying together, and it provides our children with a form for prayer that shapes their spiritual lives. It's great to have a clear pattern to follow. Especially when we're praying with a group of kids, it helps to have some words to keep us all focused! These prayers were written by wise and holy men and women, and they have been practiced by Christians for centuries. They are Catholic heirlooms! We are not only joining our prayer across the miles with others in the world praying these formal prayers, but our prayers are joining our brothers and sisters across time.

My hope is that because they've been exposed to a variety of prayer styles — formal, imaginative, meditative, and personal — my children will develop their own prayer habits and find the prayer rituals that work best for them as they enter the teen and young adult years. Recently, my teenage daughter Claire and I had a bit of a fright in the middle of the night when my husband was traveling, so we decided to pray together to calm our jitters. I suggested we pray Evening Prayer from *Shorter Christian Prayer*, but Claire asked if she could show me her prayer ritual. I tried to play it cool when she said this, but on the inside I was thinking, "Y-E-E-S! Thank you, Lord!" Claire led me through an Ignatian-style series of prayers (thanksgiving, Examen, and petitions); then we prayed an Our Father and ten Hail Marys, and we ended with a five-minute meditation. Claire apparently prays this way every night before bed. I was grateful to God that she has found a prayer life of her own. This is my hope for my children: that our family prayer life inspires them to lean on God as they mature.

And of course, there are many more formal prayers our families can practice beyond those I've shared here. There are novenas, chaplets, and litanies for different purposes. I think every family should have *Catholic Household Blessings and Prayers*, published by the United States Conference of Catholic Bishops. It has prayers for meals (including holiday meals), prayers for illness, and prayers for special occasions such as a child's birthday, First Holy Communion, first day of school, and that sort of thing.

I'm offering you all these suggestions to inspire, not overwhelm, you! If you don't have a regular family devotion time in your home, just start where you can. I developed our prayer routine over many years. Where might you start? What time of day are you all together? Pick some form of prayer that appeals to you, and just get started. If you have little kids, they might hang upside down off your couch or swing their rosaries around their necks. (Gee, how do I know that?!) God doesn't mind. He's glad you all showed up together. If you have an image in your mind of what other families look like when they're praying together, and you are irritated because your family doesn't look like that, know that no family is perfect, no child is perfectly pious, and God just wants our sincerity and love. He doesn't require perfection before he showers us with blessings.

How to Talk to Children about God

Our prayer traditions are part of the language of our great faith. That language also includes the central truths the Church teaches and the richness of Scripture and Tradition. Learning this language is a journey that lasts a lifetime, but it begins at home with you. As I already mentioned, sometimes we make the mistake of focusing solely or much too intensely on the great lists of Catholicism. We teach our children the Ten Commandments, the Seven Sacraments, the Spiritual and Corporal Works of Mercy, and such. Of course we want our children to know these things; they are truths of our Faith. But if we present our Faith like a list to be memorized, our children may never connect Church teachings to their very real but just-now budding spirituality. That spirituality needs to be nourished so it can mature. I do think we should lead with the great beauty of the Faith, as Bishop Barron suggests, including our artistic inheritance and the lives of the saints. We should teach our children doctrine, but we can consider carefully their developmental capacities and needs in how we approach it.

Tips for Ages and Stages[16]

Babies, Toddlers, and Preschoolers: When kids are really little, we can respect their limitations while recognizing their truly unique capacities. Recalling Gordon Neufeld's model for the stages of attachment from chapter 1, at this stage children are yearning to be physically close to us, the same as us, and important to us. This is how we teach our kids the language of our Faith at this stage: We keep them close, we talk about and show them how wonderful it is to be a child of God, and we show them how special they are to us and to God. They can't understand abstract theological concepts like the Trinity, transubstantiation, or baptism, but they understand hugs, kisses, and giggles! Through our faith rituals and playful, fun faith celebrations, children naturally develop tender feelings about God and "faith stuff." This is a great age to introduce a love for Mary, because little children naturally love the mommy of Jesus. You might incorporate May crownings, rosary beads, and other Marian devotions into your family faith life.

One reason to lead with the *beauty* of our Faith in our homes is that it protects and fertilizes a small child's natural gift of wonder.[17] Even though young children don't have the intellectual capacity to understand most doctrine, I do believe they have a very real experience of God drawn from their extraordinary ability to contemplate reality and to experience genuine surprise, two requirements for growing in deep faith. We don't want to extinguish these in our children. As Lydia demonstrated that day at Mass when she called out to God, children don't seem to have a hard time believing in him, looking for him, hoping for him. In presenting the Faith, we're merely helping our children find the words to describe their natural yearning for and curiosity about God.

Beginning at about age two, we do this by wondering with them about God. We can put out the nativity set on the hearth every year and enjoy looking at it, but why not talk to our children about the significance of each piece while we play with them? What did Mary say or do after the Angel Gabriel left her and she was sitting with the news that she would become the mother of God? Wonder with your little children how she felt. Was she scared or nervous? Excited and happy? There were animals in the stable to feed and dirt to clear away. Who cleaned up and brought the animals their food? Did the animals notice Jesus? When you show your four-year-old Giotto's *Sermon to the Birds* — wonder with him. I wonder what Saint Francis is saying to the birds? What do you think he was doing before he saw the birds? Why aren't the birds flying away?

We use these wondering questions to invite our children into a deeper contemplation. We aren't looking for a "right" answer. We're just trying to give them the opportunity to encounter the stories and people of our Faith in a way that excites their imaginations rather than squelching them.

School-Agers: When your child reaches age six or seven, she becomes more capable of understanding Church teaching and reflecting on it. Kids this age are ready to learn about the sacraments, Church history, the Trinity, the works of mercy, the gifts of the Holy Spirit, and such. Emotionally healthy children at this stage are looking to their parents for cues about how to feel and think about God. All your attention to family faith in the early years really pays off at this stage. The stories, rituals, and faith experiences of your child's early childhood, which were once a source of comfort and amusement, now become a source for intellectual and moral formation.[18] She will naturally begin attaching greater meaning to these stories and experiences, and she will begin asking questions about what they mean. Because their reasoning skills are developing, some kids at this stage will compare two different Gospel accounts of the same event, or they will notice a discrepancy between what they learn in a science book and what they read in the Bible. They ask hard questions! You don't have to know all the answers; you just have to be willing to walk alongside your child as she searches for the answers.

One of my favorite resources for this stage is the *Faith and Life* series published by Ignatius Press. This is a graded series of catechetical topics, with each book focusing on some particular aspect of our Faith (God the Father, Jesus, the Creed, etc.). Most of the books have images of sacred art to complement the lessons. You can get a student book, an activity book, and even a teaching guide, but just having the student book will take you a long way. Snuggle up with your child, read through a chapter, meditate on the illustrations, and say the prayers at the end. If you have several children, you can start at the beginning of the series and read from one book at a time to all your children.

I also like *Tell Me About My Catholic Faith*, which covers basic Bible stories, Church history, the sacraments, and other basic Church teachings. This colorful book is fun to read with a young child. I tend to use it as a launching tool. It helps answer some of my child's questions and prompts some more. From there, I find further resources — games, books, movies.

Teenagers: This is an exciting time to introduce your teenager to Catholic apologetics. Books like *Truth Be Told* and *Blessed Are the Bored in Spirit* by Mark Hart are written specifically for teenagers and will answer your teen's questions about Church teaching in a straightforward, appealing manner.

Most teenagers enter a stage of spiritual growth called *affiliative faith*. They want to feel a sense of belonging and connection with their church group. Kids who are peer-oriented will often either leave their childhood faith behind altogether or join the faith group of a friend. If your teenager is securely attached to you, your family remains his most influential source of faith identity, while the adults and peers at your parish begin expanding and enriching that identity. When you remain your child's secure base, when he continues to feel cherished and accepted by you, these other groups and people form a healthy part of his attachment village.

When Your Teen Has Doubts ...

Your teenager may experience a crisis of faith (by young adulthood this is probably inevitable). There's a difference between having a crisis of faith and rejecting the faith or becoming hostile toward it. Healthy children can have doubts about God and Catholicism. Their emerging individuation and increasing analytical skills make it natural for them to examine what they learned as a child or how they can incorporate it into their self-identity and personal sense of mission. Sometimes they're not sure how it all fits together and they have doubts. It can scare them, and they can feel on some level that they're betraying you or they're losing you by doubting.

It's imperative that we walk alongside our children through these doubts rather than making them feel guilty for having them. Assure your teenager that you're on her side, and you're even excited about exploring her questions! Don't be afraid to reach out to your parish priest or youth leader for help with the stumpers.[19]

I wish I could recall the author of the quote, but not long after my return to the Church, I read a quote in my missal: "Doubt is part of the path." It helped me weather the storms of the Boston sex-abuse scandal and tensions between my friends who are more traditionalist Catholics and those who are more modern. These conflicts really tested my faith in the Church. But I remembered that quote, "Doubt is part of the path." By admitting and facing my doubts about individual Catholics and even some Church teaching and policies, I was able to move through them with the guidance of the Holy Spirit and spiritual mentors. It's unsettling to have doubts, but facing my own doubts only strengthened my faith in Jesus Christ and in his Church.

Our role is to help our children know how to handle doubts, questions, and conflicts respectfully and with integrity. When we give our children permission to be honest about their doubts — about God's existence, about Church history or teaching — they move on to more mature stages of spiritual growth. From there, they are able to carve out a place for themselves in the Church, by exploring their own unique strengths and gifts.

Connecting Kids to the Mass

I couldn't write a chapter about Catholic culture and family spirituality without talking about the Mass, especially the Eucharist, given its role in my reversion. The *Catechism of the Catholic Church* describes the Eucharist as "'the source and summit of the Christian life.' 'The other sacraments, and indeed all the ecclesiastical ministries and works of the apostolate, are bound up with the Eucharist and are oriented toward it. For in the blessed Eucharist is contained the whole spiritual good of the Church, namely Christ himself, our Pasch'" (CCC 1324). Our family faith lives can also be bound up with the Eucharist and oriented toward it.

What Our Kids Need to Know

At some point, your child might say something to you like "I'm bored at Mass" or "I don't get anything from it" or "I hate it." Well, that's because they don't understand it! When they understand what's actually happening, they will drag you to Mass (or at least go with an open heart).

By the time they're teenagers, we want our kids to understand two significant things about a Catholic Mass. First, when they approach the Holy Eucharist, it appears to be a cracker and wine, but they are receiving the true Body and Blood of Christ. For kids, just explain that it's the real Body and Blood of Christ, but God knows it would be hard for us to eat human flesh and drink human blood. So in his love for us, he preserves the appearance and the taste of the bread and wine, but Christ is really present in them. It is this Real Presence that "raises the Eucharist above all the [other] sacraments."[20] We are receiving Jesus Christ the Savior into our bodies! He loves us so much that he literally gives himself to us, wholly and completely. We're talking his Body, Blood, Soul, and Divinity. Now that is not boring!

I once watched a presentation about the Mass by a fabulous old priest who had ministered in the Haight-Ashbury district in San Francisco in the 1960s (imagine lots of hippies in bellbottoms during the summer of love). He explained the graces we receive when we participate in the Eucharist. He said that the Mass is a ritual during which we basically shout together, "God, you're beautiful!" During our ritual of praise and thanksgiving, the priest blesses us multiple times, and we receive special graces through these blessings. With these graces, we may affect the life of another person, avoid an accident, or we might be blessed with a special insight about God or our life. He wondered how anybody could look sullen and bored during Mass. His explanation might help some kids appreciate that they're not meant to be passive spectators at Mass. When they're at Mass, all these special graces flow to them, fortifying them as they face the challenges and temptations of the week, and inspiring them with ideas, insights, or encounters when they most need them for understanding and fulfilling God's will.

Second, hopefully our kids understand that when they go to Mass, they are not alone: They are participating in the heavenly liturgy with the angels and saints! As the *Catechism* puts it, "by the Eucharistic celebration we already unite ourselves with the heavenly liturgy and anticipate eternal life, when God will be all in all" (CCC 1326). The Mass isn't just prefiguring the heavenly liturgy; it is part of the heavenly liturgy in real time. Christ, as the Eucharistic sacrifice, is a mediator between heaven and earth, allowing us to enter into heaven itself, worshipping with the angels and saints. When the priest exhorts the faithful to "lift up your hearts," he's not making a toast. Our hearts are raised up to heaven where our prayers, songs, and thanksgiving join those of the angels and saints, who never stop worshipping God. Wow!

More Tips for Ages and Stages

We should go to Mass to offer the best of ourselves to God, not to be entertained. But of course, we get distracted or even bored at times, especially if Father is not the most engaging homilist. If we grown-ups struggle to focus at Mass, imagine how our kids struggle. Despite our own limitations, we can help children understand the Mass better. We can offer every child, no matter her age, some gentle guidance in appreciating, respecting, and hopefully loving the Mass. Start early instilling this reverence in your kids. If your toddlers or preschoolers color or read books during Mass, encourage them to set aside those activities sometimes so they can focus on the altar, especially during the Liturgy of the Eucharist. Hold them up so they can see what's happening; whisper reverently about what the priest is doing.

You can also use a children's missal to help your child follow along. When Lydia was a preschooler, I gave her *Manners in God's House: First Prayers and First Missal*. She used it every week until she was old enough to have her own *Magnifikid* subscription, which all my children had when they were young kids. The *Magnifikid* is a lovely children's missal that comes monthly, with separate short and colorful missals for each Sunday and important feasts and solemnities. My kids were always excited when their missal packets arrived in the mail each month. The *Magnifikid* guides the child through the order of the Mass, including the Liturgy of the Word and the

Liturgy of the Eucharist. It also provides definitions for hard words and features a saint's biography and suggested morning and evening prayers every week.

To help a teenager understand and appreciate the Mass more, I highly recommend the videos on the Mass for teenagers produced by Ascension Press[21] and the book *Devotional Journey into the Mass* by Christopher Carstens. If you are blessed with a parish that offers Eucharistic adoration, begin attending with your teen or encourage her to attend with an adult mentor. The Holy Spirit works quietly sometimes, but wondrous things happen in response to prayer. My parish's youth group (all teenagers) was so devoted to the Blessed Sacrament that they were instrumental in getting monthly adoration started at our parish. You cannot teach kids to have an affection for Christ in the Eucharist. You can only pray for it, invite it, facilitate it, and model it.

"No, I'm Not Going"

What if your teenager tells you she doesn't want to attend Mass with the family? Don't be tempted to affirm her "process" by letting her stay home. Explain gently but firmly that attending Mass is not optional. This is one of those moments when you have to be a confident, calm leader for your children. You can draw out her concerns and questions; you can help her explore her faith struggles; you can connect her to adult mentors; you can share your own struggles with doubt and how you navigated through them, but your teenager should attend Mass with the rest of the family.

What if your teenager defiantly refuses to go to Mass? If your teenager is not willing to be led by you, you are looking primarily at a relationship problem, not a faith problem. So if your teenager is rude and resistant about your family faith rituals and attending Mass, begin by collecting your teenager. See the peer-orientation discussions in the discipline and empathy chapters. Win her heart back first, so she is willing to let you accompany her on her path toward maturity.

The Eucharistic Family Life

There's a direct connection between the Liturgy of the Eucharistic and our lives out in the world. When we leave Mass, blessed and filled with grace, we can go out and live a Eucharistic life as a family. A Eucharistic family life is one of thanksgiving, communion, and mission.[22]

In *thanksgiving*, we recognize the generosity of God in our everyday lives. Our homes are blessed with food and comfortable furnishings, books, clothing, games, and even pets. We have clean air, good health, and cars to drive. Many families in the world today lack these basic things that we can take for granted. We don't deserve these things any more than other families who don't have them. We see that all we have is given, not deserved, and in this way we remain more humble and less prone to irritation and resentment. It's pure grace. Our children will follow our lead in showing gratitude. If we whine and complain, if we feel entitled to possess all the latest fads and trends, our children will do the same. I'm trying to express thanks more often for things I haven't always appreciated. I've complained for years about my outdated 1960s kitchen. I'm trying more to acknowledge the gift I have in this old kitchen! It's comfortable and welcoming, and it's been the hub of family activities, conversations, and meals for many years. Our games, conversations, and meals were never ruined because my countertops are sixty years old! Thank you, God!

We can even express gratitude for the inevitable losses we experience as a family. We have to mourn before we can reach gratitude for loss. Most of us allow ourselves to mourn for great losses, like serious illness, betrayal, or death. When my father died unexpectedly in 2004, I was knocked to my knees with grief. It was thes kind of grief that digs down deep and has a good, long look around. I thought I would never be able to move on. Grace allowed me to remember my father, to feel my emptiness without him, to let go of my dreams about my children growing up with him. Then I could feel grateful for his life, for what I had learned from his death, and then I was able to move forward. Most of us allow ourselves to mourn these kinds of catastrophic losses, but there are other small losses that we easily ignore or overlook. A neighbor moving or even our baby outgrowing her newborn clothes: These are everyday losses — things that we may say are no big deal, but they still hurt a little. We can quietly acknowledge these losses, and express gratitude for what we learn through letting go.

As part of the Eucharistic life, we can help our children face their own little losses so they can learn to find gratitude in them. Life is full of mixed feelings. Some of our children are genuinely ambivalent about growing up or watching their siblings grow up. They look back over their shoulder, wistful for their smaller selves, but they are ready to move on, too. This is natural. When we acknowledge these little losses, we are able to rejoice in the adventures and experiences to come. We are grateful for both where we've been and where we're going. Experiencing and adapting to these small losses will give our kids practice, so that bigger losses are easier to handle. The little losses are necessary so we can survive the big ones.

We can support our children and allow them to have their disappointment. Eventually our children will see that happiness lives on the other side of loss. When you live the Eucharistic life, in the midst of loss, whether catastrophic or small, you begin to notice God's blessings.

The Eucharistic life also invites our family to *communion*, to intimacy. God created us to want to be known — truly, deeply known. As we've learned in prior chapters, we have a natural, intense desire to be transparent with at least one other person, to shed our masks, to open the door to our dark places, and still be loved. Only God can offer us perfect acceptance, but our earthly home is one of the few places in this life where we can be ourselves, where we can reveal our wounds, admit our mourning, and still be cherished and embraced. So, in the Eucharistic life, we can protect a child's heart so he feels safe being vulnerable and honest. This means we help siblings navigate squabbles, and we forbid cruelty in our homes. We also prioritize companionship and solidarity over outside commitments. Let's come together, let's eat, let's talk, let's see one another, let's know one another. This is communion, and Christ is among us, offering us a taste of heaven on earth.

The Eucharistic family life is also one of *mission*. Our mission as Christians is always inspired and revealed by the presence of Jesus Christ within us. When you hear or read the Mass readings (and for some family members, when you receive the Eucharist), Christ becomes immediately present to you, right then and there. He reveals himself to you and reveals more of who you are as individuals and as a whole family. At Mass, we receive the grace we need to go out and live as Christ's disciples in the world. We are called to participate in God's kingdom and the fulfillment of his promises. We can have a conversation about this as a family. What is he saying to us, revealing to us, about our mission? Even your small kids will offer their ideas!

It's easy to get into a rut, feeling like what we do doesn't matter much, especially in our parenting tasks. We wipe the same toothpaste spit out of the sink every morning, pick up the same towels off the bathroom floor every night, and push our grocery cart through the same market aisles every week. We sense Christ is present in home-run parenting moments, such as when we help a child work through a nightmare, or when we spend the morning showing our kids how to build a chicken coop. But picking up towels? Not so much.

Without the presence of Christ, we can forget that we play a role in the salvation of the world, even when we're picking up towels. Our lives are a sign of his kingdom when we act in love. Period. There aren't any limiters or qualifiers! Whether we spend our day running after toddlers, running a corporation, or running for president, Christ is present, using us to build up the Church, because his generous love is working through us. Whether we recognize our mission depends again on our gratitude. Our gratitude allows us to recognize Christ's presence, to understand his word, and to see ourselves and our mission more clearly. This calling and mission is not reserved for parents. Our children have a calling, too. The Christian life is never one only of giving; we must be willing to receive as well. In his luminous meditation on the Eucharistic life, Henri Nouwen writes: "Often mission is thought of exclusively in terms of giving, but true mission is also receiving. If it is true that the Spirit of Jesus blows where it wants, there is no person who cannot give that Spirit. In the long run, mission is possible only when it is as much receiving as giving, as much being cared for as caring."[23]

We are to receive, even from those whom we serve. We are called to reveal Christ to our children, but in humility we accept that Christ reveals himself to us through our children, even when they are not aware. We care for and give to our children, but we also allow them to care for and give to their siblings and us, in a manner that is appropriate for them.

Oh, there is so much more! I haven't even mentioned the importance of regular family confession, let alone the role of the works of mercy and the beatitudes in shaping my own family faith culture (and keeping my attitude in check). I invite you to visit my website (kimcameronsmith.com) where you will find links to my articles and podcasts about living your family faith joyfully every day. There are many other blogs written by parents with a special gift for celebrating the liturgical seasons at home, and I encourage you to check in with them frequently.[24] Two books I recommend for your bookshelf are Kendra Tierney's *Catholic All Year Compendium* and Greg and Lisa Popcak's *Discovering God Together*.

I think we have a good start here, though: the beauty of our Faith, real heroes, family prayer, and the graces of the Eucharistic life. As we build our home faith culture, our children can begin to experience the peace and abundance available to them when they live in friendship with Jesus Christ. We can never guarantee our children's paths of faith, and we can't force our children to believe what we believe, but we can create a home life that is full of sacred invitation and beauty. Hopefully they will experience our Catholic faith as so joyful and grace-filled that they can't imagine living any other way!

CHAPTER SEVEN

A Strong Marriage

*This is my commandment, that you love one
another as I have loved you.*
JOHN 15:12

To love at all is to be vulnerable.
C. S. LEWIS, THE FOUR LOVES

My first date with Philip was memorable partly because I had no idea we were on a date. That's right. No clue. We had been friends for two years. During those two years, it had never dawned on me that he had any interest in me beyond our sincere but quiet friendship. So when he asked me to see a movie with him, I figured the arrangement was the same as it had been many times before. (Though he did point out later that we'd always been out with our group of friends and not alone.) He showed up in his dress pants and one good sweater. I was in my sweats because I'd just come home from the gym. I finally realized Philip's intention at the end of the date when he put his arm around my shoulder to help me cross the street ... and left it there when we got to the other side. I was speechless. At least in my head I was speechless. I'm sure we talked the rest of the walk home, but I was utterly befuddled, distracted, and delighted.

His friends (and even a few of mine) told me later that I must have been blind; they all knew how he felt about me. But I guess I didn't read him well. Nearly twenty-five years after that surprising first date, many things about Philip remain mysterious for me, but I think I've learned a few things about him and how we can avoid tripping over each other too much on our journey together through life.

One thing I've learned: My marriage models for my children how to treat others in intimate relationships. If we treat our children with warmth and acceptance, but fail to model such generosity with our spouse, our children will still grow up missing one of the most significant pieces of the relationship puzzle. So in this chapter, I'd like to explore how spouses can nourish and strengthen their own unique bond while growing their family into a community of love. I'll share what I've learned about the sacramental power of marriage and how that power can carry us through rough patches.

The Great News about Catholic Marriage

When Philip and I became engaged and it was time to make wedding arrangements, we were sent to a weekend Pre-Cana retreat. I wasn't really sure what Pre-Cana was all about or whether it was worth going. By the time we left the retreat, I understood clearly what it was about, and I was so glad we went.

We learned about many things that weekend. The retreat leaders led all the couples in reflecting together on several issues, things they felt every couple should discuss before their wedding, including financial issues, natural family planning, communication, and work-family balance. Philip and I come from very different cultural and socioeconomic backgrounds, so before that weekend, I did wonder about our compatibility. But discussing the retreat topics with Philip helped me see how well-suited we were for each other. On the questionnaires, we scored very high in compatibility because we had the same values, expectations, and hopes as we envisioned our future together. I had confidence that we could weather storms together because we were in the same boat.

The topic that struck me most that weekend was the Church's teaching on the Sacrament of Matrimony and the spiritual effects of marital love. I had never heard it before, and I was drawn immediately to its mystery, depth, and beauty. I think if a bride and groom understand and appreciate the spiritual significance of their wedding day, they will focus much more on the Church ceremony than on the party afterwards.

The Sacramental Couple

Marriage between a man and woman is a transhistorical, cross-cultural practice. In other words, people everywhere have been entering into marriage throughout history. It has always served important social, economic, and political purposes — societies were made and perpetuated through the strength of family units. Jesus Christ elevated marriage to the level of a sacrament because he wanted to make clear that marriage not only strengthens society, but the whole spiritual Body of Christ (CCC 1601).

In a Catholic wedding (the Rite of Marriage), through the "epiclesis" of the sacrament (when the priest invokes the Holy Spirit during his blessing of the couple), "the spouses receive the Holy Spirit as the communion of love of Christ and the Church." The Holy Spirit is the seal of the marital covenant between the two spouses (CCC 1624), and their covenant is swept up into God's covenant with mankind (CCC 1639). It's important to note that this covenant is made even when a Catholic is marrying a non-Catholic, as long they are married in the Church. You are still in a Catholic marriage under the seal of the covenant.

Like all sacraments, weddings are a ritual of remembrance, celebration, and hope. On our wedding day, Philip and I marked the history we had already shared together: We recalled the first day we met, our first date (that I didn't know was a date until the end of the date!), the many hours we talked about books and ideas, and our friendship that had grown even before we became a "couple." As we stood before our family and friends, all gussied up and smiling until our faces hurt, we also affirmed our love and commitment to one another, how we cherished one another in the present moment. And we marked with hope the future we would have together. We promised to welcome children, to nourish one another and our children with love, to be faithful to each other and to these promises through thick and thin.

However, the Church perceives in one couple's marriage more than that particular couple's past, present, and future. She sees something mysterious and profound: She sees the Church's own past, present, and future. John Paul II wrote that:

> Spouses are therefore the permanent reminder to the Church of what happened on the Cross; they are for one another and for the children witnesses to the salvation in which the sacrament makes them sharers. Of this salvation event marriage, like every sacrament, is a memorial, actuation and prophecy: "As a *memorial*, the sacrament gives them the grace and duty of commemorating the great works of God and of bearing witness to them before their children. As *actuation*, it gives them the grace and duty of putting into practice in the present, towards each other and their children, the demands of a love which forgives and redeems. As *prophecy*, it gives them the grace and duty of living and bearing witness to the hope of the future encounter with Christ."[1]

We, as husband and wife, stand as a reminder of Christ's salvific work — his suffering and sacrifice, his willingness to give all for the sake of love. And not just on our wedding day, but every day of our lives together. By our very lives, we bear witness to the great work of God in the past, the divine love and forgiveness available to us today, and our hope of entering heaven in the future.

You may feel like this is all very romantic, and not at all reflective of what you're dealing with in real life. How can you serve as a sign for the Church when you're busy raising children and paying down a mortgage? That's part of the point, though. Jesus lived an ordinary human life for thirty years, hidden away, doing all the normal things a poor Jewish boy or man would do back then, including hard work, gathering with family and friends in celebration and mourning, and working through squabbles with neighbors. He entered the messiness of human experience to redeem these activities, to help us understand the role they play in the story of our personal salvation. For Catholic couples, our real, everyday experiences matter because that's where God reveals the whole truth about marriage, and it's where we work out our own salvations.

Thankfully, we are given not only a duty to stand as a divine sign, but also the grace to meet our duty. God gives us special graces on our wedding day that allow our marriage to become an instrument of sanctification and evangelization — the best wedding gift ever! The *Catechism* puts it like this:

> "By reason of their state in life and of their order, [Christian spouses] have their own special gifts in the People of God." This grace proper to the Sacrament of Matrimony is intended to perfect the couple's love and to strengthen their indissoluble unity. By this grace they "help one another to attain holiness in their married life and in welcoming and educating their children." *Christ is the source of this grace. ...* Christ dwells with them, gives them the strength to take up their crosses and so follow him, to rise again after they have fallen, to forgive one another, to bear one another's burdens, to

"be subject to one another out of reverence for Christ,"
and to love one another with supernatural, tender, and
fruitful love. (CCC 1641–42)

Through the *sacramental* graces of marriage, we receive the
actual graces that we need to live a joyful, sacred life with our
spouse. We are empowered to become an uncommon sign of
love to the world. We couldn't do this on our own, but with
God's grace, we can move to continually deeper levels of loving. Christ dwells with you and your spouse, helping you as a
couple (1) to become more holy through your marriage (not
despite it!); (2) to love one another with supernatural power;
(3) to bear with one another's inevitable shortcomings; and (4)
to raise your children to become disciples of Christ.

For those of us who have been called to the vocation of
matrimony, our marriage is our path to sainthood. Because of
Christ's sacrifice, we have been provided the power to make
our way with confidence. God wants us to experience joy,
peace, and the fullness of love in our marriages.

The Safe Haven Marriage

With Christ's example and the guidance of the Holy Spirit, we
can realize the graces of sacramental marriage.[2] Despite our
ordinary lives, we can experience uncommon contentment
and peace as husband and wife. I have some thoughts to point
you in the right direction, some little tips for helping you tap
into the graces of marriage. These suggestions have nothing
to do with changing our spouse or getting him or her to do
stuff to make us happier. Instead, they help refocus our own
attitudes and perceptions. My tips are all rooted in our natural
drive for connection to our husband or wife. When things are
going as God intended, we are deepening our connection.

Marriage and Attachment

During his career, John Bowlby, the father of attachment theory, came to believe that the dynamics of attachment that he observed in children and their mothers applied similarly to adult relationships. He began investigating this theory as early as World War II. He conducted a study of war widows, and he discovered that these women exhibited behavior patterns similar to those of children when faced with separation from their attachment figure. He tried to disseminate his research, but he was soundly ignored.

After Bowlby's death in 1990, social psychologists Phil Shaver and Cindy Hazan confirmed Bowlby's theory: The key principles of attachment theory apply to adult relationships. Their discoveries in several studies led to a revolution in how we understand the nature of attachment in marriage.[3] From birth to death, we long for what Bowlby called *effective dependency*. We naturally seek out and stay close to a select few loved ones who serve as a safe haven from the storms of life and bruising blows of the world. After God, our spouse is meant to be our primary safe haven.[4]

Both spouses naturally hunger for closeness, connection, and protection in their marriage. When our spouse is our safe haven, he or she also becomes our secure base from which we can go out and explore the world, just as children do with their parents. When we know our spouse values and understands us, when we're confident he'll protect and defend us, we have greater courage, creativity, and enthusiasm as we encounter new experiences and opportunities.

Connecting with our spouse is harder for some of us than connecting with our kids. But we all want to be seen, cherished, understood, and held close by our husband or wife. All of us. However, depending on our adult attachment style (which I introduced in chapter 1), we may not be completely free to accept and return our spouse's bids of intimacy and vulnerability. The rules we've internalized about our own value and the safety of others can create more or less healthy patterns of relating to our spouse.

Secure adults are comfortable with physical and emotional closeness, and they believe they can count on their spouse. They don't mind when their spouse leans on them for support. They tend to give their spouse the benefit of the doubt in conflict, and they get over hurts relatively easily. **Anxious-preoccupied** spouses tend to regard their spouse highly and themselves negatively, so they are insecure in the marriage. They fear that if their spouse really knew them, the spouse would reject them. They are the long-suffering martyrs who don't speak up for themselves, but they become enraged after they get tired of giving themselves completely with little in return. They create a "pursue, then reject" dynamic in the marriage. **Avoidant** spouses are loner types; they often seem cold and distant. They don't like any perceived demands or neediness from their spouse. They avoid situations that will elicit strong emotions.

All marriages experience periods of disconnection and conflict, but when one or both spouses carry attachment wounds, the patterns of conflict can become increasingly destructive. These spouses tend to blame each other for the disconnection and mistrust in the marriage. Both you and your spouse want the same thing: to belong, to be understood, to be accepted, to be loved unconditionally. Even if a spouse appears cold and detached, he wants this. Some spouses have old injuries that create "spark points" that trigger defensiveness or alarm in particular situations or conversations. These spark points cause them to turn away from the other spouse, because they perceive a threat, even if none exists.

It was more difficult for me to get past my attachment issues with Philip than with my kids. Why didn't I read Philip well when he was interested in me romantically? I couldn't recognize the softness and safety of real love. It took me a long time to understand it. I struggled with emotional vulnerability and defensiveness in our marriage for many years. I'm still a work in progress, but Philip and I finally have come to a place of emotional peace together (at least on most days!).[5] While we have far from a perfect marriage, Philip and I do find a safe haven in each other. We're in sync.

I've discovered that when you're at peace and in sync as a couple, you can get on with growing together rather than picking up the pieces. This doesn't mean we don't have bad days, but when we have them, we know we'll get through them together. God wants a safe haven marriage for you, too, and if I can be healed enough to thrive in my marriage, anybody can.

Nourishing Deep Connection

The first step toward healing is to turn toward your spouse instead of away from him or her. You have to make a decision to take a risk and give your heart to your spouse. Pray for a soft heart; call on Mary, Undoer of Knots (see chapter 1). Here I'd like to offer you some thoughts that might help you move toward your spouse, so that hopefully you can find a safe harbor in him or her. In this section, I will share some habits of connection that you can practice during times you're in tune and at peace with your spouse (basically, when you're not having a conflict). Then, in the following section, I'd like to offer you some tried-and-true habits for managing conflict in a healthier way than what you perhaps witnessed growing up or are living with now.

Spouses can develop habits of connection that deepen the roots of their attachment to each other. Recall the six ways of attaching which I introduced in chapter 1: proximity, sameness, belonging, loyalty, significance, love, and being known. These attachment needs apply to all relationships, including married couples. Within all humans, there exists one yearning for connection, but six ways of seeking and finding it.

Proximity

Connecting through proximity with our spouse means we enjoy spending time in each other's company. For Catholics, the physical intimacy of marriage (sex) is a joyful, holy renewal of our wedding vows. This is an important way for us to connect physically, but there are other ways — little daily habits that can create a natural rapport between us. Kids have their daily rituals and routines that provide them a sense of safety and comfort; familiar rhythms for coming together as a couple will do the same for mom and dad.

Make time to connect every day through special relationship rituals with your spouse. You probably do this already without thinking about it. Philip and I both enjoy talking, so we have many talking rituals. When he returns home from work, Philip always finds me to say hello and catch up. He's a night owl and I'm a morning person, but I seek him out at night before I go to bed to have a goodnight chat. During these rituals, we might just talk about the kids, an interesting article one of us read, or something we heard on the radio. But we also talk about deeper concerns, such as our parents or struggles in our friendships. Our talking rituals ground our marriage and create regular and natural invitations for physical closeness.

Many couples have date-night rituals that foster physical closeness. Terrific idea, but I don't think a couple should feel pressured to have regular date nights out if it won't work for their family. When our children were all young, Philip and I didn't go out on many dates. Maybe two or three times a year. We never wanted to leave our infants with a babysitter, and babysitters were expensive. Just as some people enjoy "staycations" more than away vacations, Philip and I preferred date nights at home. We found inexpensive and fun ways to "play" as a couple. Board games, puzzles, and reading together are some of our favorite at-home date nights. When our youngest was an infant, Philip introduced me to science fiction film and television. We would watch an episode of *Battlestar Galactica* while I nursed the baby, and sometimes (. . . usually) we had to parent ourselves and firmly send ourselves to bed even though we wanted to watch "just one more" episode.

Now our older kids can babysit for us, so we go out more often (but probably not as often as some couples). In our town, we have a wonderful, old movie theater that has couches and tables in the screening rooms instead of regular movie chairs. The theater even serves dinner during the movie. This is one of our favorite date-night destinations, probably because it fuels our talking rituals! Our parish has regular date nights for couples that include dinner and a speaker; we try not to miss these gatherings. We also like bowling and trying unusual restaurants. But we're still mostly homebodies. We like to be at home together, and that's okay.

Sameness

If we want to deepen our connection beyond physical closeness, we need to have something in common. Fortunately, spouses have a natural connection in their shared history, and hopefully shared values, goals, and expectations. I think couples should regularly reflect together on their hopes and dreams for the future. Having that shared vision binds us together in the same way our shared history does. The work Philip and I did at that Pre-Cana retreat, in which we enjoyed talking about our future and what we both imagined and hoped for in it, stayed with us. We still enjoy talking about our dreams together, and it's also fun to look back and reflect on how our life together has unfolded compared to what we expected. I know he would agree that we're more fulfilled than we imagined, and we've had many unexpected adventures and blessings. God's care and providence for us as a couple are unmistakable.

Don't forget to connect through shared interests. You likely shared some common hobbies or activities when you met, but it's easy to forget about them when children come along or we get caught up in the busyness of life. Did you hike together? Fish? Volunteer? Camp? You can continue to enjoy those interests together with kids in tow, or you can explore new ones.

Naturally, some of the ideas you come up with will overlap with the play rituals mentioned earlier, and for good reason: Rituals both draw us together and create a shared identity. Really they go hand in hand.

Although we are different in some ways, Philip and I enjoy many shared interests, including books, devotional groups at our parish, and hiking. We both really love debating about a wide variety of topics, from politics to the right way to launder whites! We don't really understand why some people think debating is negative and destructive; for us it's downright fun. You just have to respect boundaries and counterargue with evidence, not personal attacks.

Philip and I both enjoy working together on house projects. We never imagined we could ever afford a house when we moved to the San Francisco Bay Area, but we managed it. We both enjoy the process of planning our projects together, picking out materials, working together on the projects, and admiring the results. We've found ways to make our home warm and welcoming even on a tight budget. Personally, I think the home improvement store is very romantic! This may not be your thing, but I think it's good for us because we both tend to be too much in our heads. (I also think Philip is really attractive when he uses power tools. Just sayin'.)

When you have small babies, sometimes your sameness comes in the shared craving for sleep. That's fine! When you view parenting as a mutual vocation and divine calling, sharing laughter and confusion in the occasional turbulent waters of raising kids will draw you together.

Loyalty
In order for our marriage to be a safe haven, we need to protect each other from outside threats. When our spouse faces hardships at work or in relationships, we can offer our support and comfort. Our spouse needs to know we are on his side, no matter what. One of the most wounding things a spouse can

do is to belittle the other spouse in front of friends or family. Even if we don't always agree with our spouse, we need to stand beside him and defend him against gossip or meanness. In fidelity, spouses hold each other very dear. We look out for each other; when we are in distress or in a jam, we know exactly who has our back.

When you marry somebody, in many ways you're wandering into the wilderness together, and you promise to stick together no matter what you encounter "out there." Ideally, the permanence of the marriage commitment gives us a sense of trust that we'll be a team even when things get hard. So, in loyalty, we don't threaten to leave the marriage, even during our darkest moments when our doubts and fears have moved us to high alert. Both spouses need to know they'll stick together through thick and thin.

Significance

Now we're moving into deeper levels of attachment that require increasingly greater vulnerability. Some spouses have a lot in common, but they still don't feel very important to each other. We can increase a sense of significance by prioritizing our relationship. It's so easy to slip into a routine in which we're basically living parallel lives, only interacting to go over domestic "business." Every couple goes through such days or periods, but it's important eventually to bring the balance back and remind each other that the relationship is important.

I've always delighted in hearing about the endearing, little things spouses do to make each other feel treasured. I heard of a husband who brought his wife "the flower of the day" every day from their garden; sometimes it was a single bud, while at other times it was a whole bouquet. My in-laws have a big stuffed tiger on their bed. Every day the spouse who makes the bed arranges this lion in humorous poses to make the other spouse laugh. These are examples of ways we can make our spouse feel treasured in meaningful or playful ways. They create real warmth and rapport. Such gestures don't require a great deal of time; only attention.

Another important way to help your spouse feel significant is to try things he's interested in even if you aren't particularly keen on them. Philip and I learned at Pre-Cana that it's a sign of a generous heart when you can learn to enjoy life in new ways because of your spouse's ideas and interests. That was very wise advice. You might be pleasantly surprised. Because of Philip, I now have a deeper appreciation for science fiction, ballroom dancing, and his favorite animal: worms!

We can also strengthen significance by treating each other with great regard, even when we're irritated or frustrated with each other. Yes, this can be challenging. I offer some tips below for handling conflict in productive, healthy ways.

Love (Emotional Intimacy)

Going even deeper, our marriage becomes a safe haven when we experience emotional intimacy: an authentic, mutual caring and concern. Ideally, both spouses are free to share what they are dealing with personally and what they are concerned about in the marriage, without fear of judgment or rejection. This requires trust and vulnerability. Many of us resist real emotional intimacy, because we can't bear the risk of being hurt. But vulnerability builds strong marriages. The more vulnerable we can be together, the more we can trust one another, and the stronger our marriage will become. We all long to have this kind of connection with our spouses.

If your spouse can't be that person for you, you can still be that person for him. Accept his gestures of openness. When he risks revealing his heart in any way, try to offer your full attention and interest, at least most of the time. Don't criticize or shame; invite the vulnerability with acceptance and understanding. Just as we can empathize with children even when we don't agree with their choices, we can try to see our spouse's perspective and respect his intentions.

Being Known (Psychological Intimacy)

We all long to have that one person in our life with whom we can be open and honest. This is psychological intimacy, and it's the deepest level of connection we can experience with another person. Many people never experience it in their marriage. For the anxious-preoccupied spouse, they resist revealing their real opinions and thoughts for fear they'll be rejected or criticized. They tend to say what they think the spouse will want to hear. They "go along to get along," but in doing so, they feel lonely and invisible. Avoidant spouses believe on a deep level that loneliness is better than judgment, so they convince themselves that they don't need anyone to understand them.

In order to nourish psychological intimacy, we have to give each other space to express our views, ideas, and opinions. While it can be a challenge, we can nourish psychological intimacy in our marriage by avoiding toxic communication habits like criticizing and contempt. I talk more about this in the next section. We can't possibly agree with everything our spouse thinks. But this makes marriage interesting! Thank you, God, that Philip isn't my clone, with thoughts exactly like mine, but somebody who continues to surprise me with his ideas and opinions.

If you are aware that you or your spouse carries attachment wounds, it's imperative that these vulnerabilities be acknowledged. Seek professional help if necessary. If a wife has a fear of abandonment and the husband has an aversion to neediness, this is a recipe for disaster, unless they both recognize these vulnerabilities in one another and accommodate each other with greater care and respect. The needy spouse may need to give the other spouse some space, and the distant spouse may need to find ways to move closer to his spouse through the six paths of connection. As long as they are moving more toward one another rather than away, they are growing together.

Deepening our connection to our spouse is mostly about creating a sense of knowing, companionship, and kinship.

This doesn't require grand vacations and expensive gifts. This is really a quiet path paved with small acts of love: noticing your wife's favorite tea, tucking a note into your husband's jacket pocket, turning toward your wife and smiling when she tells you a joke, a hand on the shoulder when your husband has a bad day. Small acts, but they have a big impact on our hearts.

Learn How to Fight

Every couple will have conflict, but it doesn't have to destroy your marriage. Fighting isn't even a sign that you have a bad marriage. John Gottman, the director of the Gottman Institute (the famed "Seattle Love Lab"), found after many decades of research that it's not the *content* of the fighting (what we're fighting about) that predicts the strength or weakness of a relationship, but how we *manage* the fighting.[6] Healthy couples argue, but they do two things that set them apart from less healthy couples: (1) they avoid the four most destructive communication habits, and (2) they recognize the signs when they're reaching their "freak-out threshold" during conflict.

Avoiding the Four Deadly Horsemen of Marriage

Particular styles of negative communication are so lethal to marriage that Gottman dubbed them "The Four Deadly Horsemen of Marriage." The first deadly horseman is **criticism**. It's okay to complain to your spouse, but criticism is very different from complaints. A complaint focuses on a specific problem in a direct, productive way without being critical: "I'm really disappointed that you didn't do the dishes last night. Can you do them before you leave for work?" Criticism focuses on the spouse's character and tends to be global in nature: "You are so inconsiderate. You never follow through when I ask you to do something." A complaint focuses on an *issue*, while a criticism attacks the spouse's *character*. Criticism commonly uses words such as "you never" or "you always": "You never remember to take out the trash"; "You always put yourself before our family." What we intend as a complaint can turn into criticism when we add a little zinger such as "You're just like your mother" or "What's wrong with you?" Heads up: anxious-preoccupied adults might take an honest, well-meaning complaint as criticism, so if you or your spouse are anxious-preoccupied, it's important that the other spouse understands this and offers extra reassurance during a complaint.

Constant criticism can weaken trust between spouses. We don't feel safe with each other. Apparently, women are more likely to be chronic criticizers than men. I've noticed that sometimes I start off with an honest, well-intentioned complaint to Philip, but I end up sounding critical. Gottman suggests a three-part formula to keep a complaint from turning into criticism: (1) State how you feel ("I'm disappointed"); (2) about a specific, narrow situation ("that you didn't do the dishes last night"); and (3) what you need/want/prefer now ("Can you do them before you leave for work?").[7] This advice really helps me stay focused if I can remember it. Basically, we need to focus on what we need, and not on how our husband or wife is bad or defective in some way.

The second deadly horseman of marriage is **contempt**. Contempt is criticism on steroids. One spouse displays a sense of superiority over the other spouse. Contempt is seen in sarcasm, cynicism, name-calling, eye-rolling, sneering, mockery, and hostile humor. The target of contempt feels belittled, and over time, they can come to believe what the contemptuous spouse is saying. Avoidant adults can fall into a bad habit of speaking contemptuously to their spouses. Contempt is extremely destructive and defeating. You can't resolve a relationship problem once contempt enters the conversation, because one spouse is basically saying he's disgusted by the other spouse. Gottman says contemptuous communication is the single biggest predictor of divorce. We can insulate our marriage from contempt by creating a marriage culture of benevolence and appreciation, as seen in the connection habits above. When you're busy falling more deeply in love through proximity, sameness, significance, loyalty, love, and being known, it's very hard to feel or express any kind of contempt.

The third deadly horseman is **defensiveness**. Many spouses become defensive in response to a spouse who's criticizing them. One spouse says, "Why can't you come home on time? I'm not your babysitter," so the defensive spouse says, "I don't think you're my babysitter. I was at work making money to put a roof over your head." The attacked spouse shows righteous indignation in an attempt to ward off a perceived attack. This response is self-protective in nature, but becoming defensive makes the problem worse. The defensive spouse tends to overstate matters in his own defense, so he ends up blaming the other spouse in some way, who responds with yet more criticism. The defensive spouse is basically saying, "It's not me; it's you." Then, the other spouse says, "Oh no, buddy, it's definitely you." And around and around.

If we want to break the defensiveness habit, we can practice the virtue of humility and admit our part in the conflict. Can we recognize where we went wrong at all? We can change the direction of the criticism-defensiveness train by saying something like, "Yep, I'm home late. I'm sorry. You've had a long day. Can I make you some tea?" I used to complain frequently to Philip about his long showers. (Sometimes these were reasonable complaints, but at other times they were definitely criticisms.) He's been taking very long showers since we were married, and I've complained about them every few months, so that's a lot of showers and a lot of complaining. His showers have never gotten any shorter, so I'm not sure why I continued complaining! He often became a bit defensive, trying to explain why he has to take long showers. He said it helped his allergies, so I offered to buy him a facial steamer. He said it helped him think, so I suggested sarcastically (ah, contempt!) that he should get out of the shower and go to work where he's paid to think. His excuses just irritated me. For more than two decades we were on the "Criticism-Defense Express" bound for nowhere. I think this dynamic went on for so long because I found it challenging to come up with better and better reasons why he shouldn't be taking long showers. One day I was very excited about my latest snazzy argument, which had something to do with saving money (which I knew he would appreciate). I pitched him my new evidence, and guess what he said? "I know. I wish I didn't take such long showers. It's just one of my 'things.'"

What? Hang on. Where'd this come from? I was not prepared for that! Well, shoot. I have my "things," too, so I know what he means. I drink too much coffee. I spend too much money on moisturizer. My minivan is a mess, with stickers on the windows, crumbs under the seat, and ice cream stains on the ceiling. I have my "things," so I can give him some room to have his "things" too. So I don't complain about (or criticize) his showers anymore. I will let him work out the shower problem on his own. What shifted was that he acknowledged his showers were probably too long. Instead of becoming defensive, he acknowledged where he might be wrong. When you change from being defensive to being humble and admitting your part, your spouse may not automatically stop complaining, but your conversation will definitely move in a more positive, productive direction.

Stonewalling is the fourth deadly horseman of marriage. Stonewalling happens when one spouse shuts the other one out and withdraws from the discussion. They don't criticize; they don't show contempt; they don't defend themselves. They just shut down and turn inward, leaving the other spouse alone emotionally and sometimes even physically. It's very destructive because it sends the message to the other spouse that "you're not important" or "you're not worth fighting for."

Often stonewallers become emotionally overwhelmed, and they don't know how to handle it without exploding in anger, so they withdraw. They stonewall to avoid their own tempers, but they're also avoiding their marriages. Apparently, men are more likely to be stonewallers than women. One alternative to stonewalling is to call a time out. Just say to your spouse, "I need to take a break." This allows your body to calm down so you can talk rationally, but you aren't rejecting your husband or wife. See my discussion of managing your freak-out threshold below.

If a stonewaller is married to an anxious-preoccupied spouse, they might fall into a fiery pursue-withdraw dynamic. The anxious spouse will pursue the stonewaller because of her own anxiety about rejection, but she needs to give the stonewaller some space to get his head together. They should talk this over during a calm, connected conversation, so they can come to an understanding about how they can both get their needs met during a conflict.

All relationships, even very healthy ones, have conflict. While unavoidable, we can handle conflict in ways that help us grow as a couple. The four deadly horsemen are so destructive because they set up a lose-lose dynamic. We have to turn toward each other, with an attitude of emotional openness, even when we're disagreeing about something.

The *Catechism* tells us: "God who created man out of love also calls him to love — the fundamental and innate vocation of every human being. For man is created in the image and likeness of God who is himself love. Since God created him man and woman, their mutual love becomes an image of the absolute and unfailing love with which God loves man" (CCC 1604).

Our connection to God and to one another is the most fundamental aspect of our humanity. To be disconnected from love and how to find it with our spouse is nothing short of tragic. In the *Catechism*, it also says that while the love between husband and wife is an image of the love God has for mankind, it's become disordered because of original sin (CCC

1607). In the Garden of Eden, the communion between man and woman was ruptured because of their "mutual recriminations." What is mutual recrimination? They *blamed* each other for their problems! That's exactly what Gottman is warning us against. Don't blame each other; don't get defensive; don't criticize.

Spousal love is meant to offer us a safe haven from the storms of life. Love is our fortress, designed to provide emotional protection so we can cope with the wounding that happens out in the world. God knows we need a safe haven in each other. When our spousal relationship becomes the source of the storms, the cause of the wounding, we have nowhere to go. We suffer. What's more, our children see this as normative, that this is what love is like, that this is what you should do when you care about somebody. You criticize, push away, put down, distance yourself. Division is a tool of the devil. He will look for ways into your marriage to separate you from your spouse. Fight back and protect your connection. We all want to have somebody with whom we can reveal our hearts without being crushed. If we can develop healthy habits in conflict, we are modeling for our kids how to handle their own conflicts. Not by attacking or defending, but by protecting the relationship even while being honest.

Recognizing Your Freak-Out Threshold

In healthy marriages, spouses offer one another a sense of safety, emotional availability, and sensitivity, even when they're disagreeing.[8] They turn toward each other, not against. One of the obstacles to remaining connected during conflict is that we become so emotionally charged that we can't think straight. Sometimes your brain doesn't know what to do during a conflict with your spouse, because you're flooded with adrenaline. This is the "freak-out threshold" that I introduced in chapter 1. Your higher, rational brain goes offline, and you're in fight-or-flight mode. This takes us down a low road, where we turn in on ourselves and can no longer engage in a healthy way with our spouse. We don't care about connection to our spouse at this point.

Specific stressors or triggers can wear us down so that we're no longer capable of second-guessing our impulsive thoughts; we just act on them. To remain engaged emotionally during conflict, we have to recognize and manage our emotional limits; we have to avoid allowing our stress to rise above a manageable level. Again, Gottman found that managing our marital conflicts in a healthy way has nothing to do with what we're actually fighting about; the problem comes when we disconnect and turn away from each other. When we begin to perceive the love of our lives as the enemy who needs to be put in his place, we've hit the low road.

We don't have to take the low road, ever. If we gain a simple awareness of our stress levels while we're still thinking straight, we can make a choice to take the high road before it's too late. To remain on the high road, you don't have to sit in a lotus pose humming mantras about peace and harmony. In fact, it's possible to remain emotionally engaged with your spouse even when you're angry or irritated. You just have to pay attention to your emotional intensity and find strategies for reversing course when you're nearing your threshold.

Most of the time we probably feel very warmly toward our spouse and we're quietly engaged with him or her. But pay attention to what happens when some stress is added to the mix. First, your spouse forgets it's your anniversary. You let it roll off you; no problem, you tell yourself. He's been busy. But beneath the surface it bothers you. Then he points out an imperfection in your outfit, intending to be helpful. You say thank you, but inside it stings. You begin to think of sarcastic things you could say, but you don't. You're getting irritated, but you're still in control. Maybe now your kids are awake, but your husband doesn't notice and continues looking down at his phone while you're running around trying to get them ready for school. Now, you're really starting to get ticked off. You begin to feel the rising tension below the surface, and you know you won't be able to hold your tongue for long. Once we reach this point, we have a harder time managing stress without an attacking type energy (yelling, blaming, threatening). You don't want to get to a place where you know you're going to lose it. If we go beyond our personal freak-out threshold, we're no longer in control; we'll say things we later regret. This is where the virtue of prudence comes in. You have to know what is too much for you. When you pass your threshold, you lose your filters and you will fail to act with virtue.

When you approach your threshold, you need a break. How this looks will depend on the situation. In all situations, leaning on God in prayer is powerful. See my thoughts in chapter 1 on the Mary, Undoer of Knots prayer and the Rosary, and how these devotions helped me with my own emotional turbulence. If you tend to release frustration through talking, you might call a friend or write in a prayer journal. If you tend to release frustration physically, you might just need to fold some laundry (very vigorously) or prune your rose bushes (very firmly). Better yet, fold laundry or prune bushes while praying! There are ways you can raise your freak-out threshold so that you're able to remain calm for longer under more stressful conditions. An active prayer life and developing the habits of connection (the six ways of attaching above) with your spouse during good times will help you develop greater patience and self-control, because you'll have a foundation of trust and rapport.

This is a good place to point out that it's okay to be honest about things that hurt you before you approach your freak-out limit. In my narrative above, the spouse forgot the anniversary, let his wife handle the morning routine, and was basically disengaged. Being a loving, self-giving spouse doesn't require us to be a doormat. Sometimes we will bear wrongs quietly, and we know in prayer that this is what we should do; but at other times, the right thing to do is to say something gently that our spouse needs to hear. If we talk about these things right away, we clear the air while we're still connected.

Remember Your "Original Vision" of Your Spouse

If you've been married more than a year, you know that inevitably the "warm sea-scented beaches" and "fiery ringlets"[9] of early love eventually change. It's very normal and healthy to transition from starry-eyed love to a comfortable attachment. But let's never forget why we married each other in the first place.

As the months and years pass, it's easy to start focusing on the little things about our spouse that irritate us (*Why can't he put the forks in the right spot in the cutlery tray?*). We may tuck away in our memories the hurts (even the small ones) perpetrated upon us (*Why does she keep making sweet potatoes when she knows I hate them?*). Perhaps, before we know it, those irritations and hurts build up and we feel emotionally distant from the same person who once inspired us to doodle floaty hearts on café napkins. We may even wonder whether we ever really knew this person we married. Instead of comfortable attachment, we transition to disconnection or even resentment.

English writer Charles Williams (pal to C. S. Lewis and the often-forgotten member of the Inklings literary group) made a subtle observation about the nature of mature love that I try to keep in mind, especially on those days when I encounter a few thorns in my relationship with Philip. Williams conceded that young love has to change in order for a relationship to mature and endure, but he believed that we overlook too easily the significance of the original revelation or vision we had of our beloved.[10] Maybe, just maybe, the most important quality in them is the thing that awakened love in us in the first place — despite the truth of our experiences since then. The present hurts can be true, but the mistake is to allow those hurts to cloud our original vision of our spouse.

God works in these revelations of early love. The "something special" you and your spouse saw in each other revealed what you two could become together. The many graces of marriage can flow through those qualities if we don't allow cynicism to distract us. Do you remember the first weeks and months after you began dating your spouse? For some, those early signs of love are intoxicating; for others, it's all a little frightening. At some point, though, you realized something was different about *this* one. For me, Philip's kindness and honesty attracted and fascinated me most. He treated me the way he treated everyone we knew: with openness, acceptance, and genuine interest in who we were and what we thought. When Philip talks to you, you have a keen sense that your presence is important to him, and that what you have to say is interesting to him. He's a gifted conversationalist and a loyal friend. I love these things about him.

So, what drew you to your spouse? What made him or her different from every other man or woman you knew? What about him or her stirred something new in you, something you had never experienced before? Williams reminds us that those early experiences of our spouse probably reveal a central truth about who they are and what makes them unique and unrepeatable, and that central truth still exists within them today.

Philip isn't perfect. He has made mistakes in our marriage (and I've made more); there have been moments of pain between us. Remember the cultural and background differences that I was concerned about at our Pre-Cana retreat? Philip is European (he's a New Zealander who grew up in England), while I'm American. He leans toward the Democratic platform, while I lean toward the Republican platform. He grew up in a stable, loving family, while I grew up in economically challenging circumstances in an unstable family life with many divorces and remarriages. Well, it turns out those differences do matter. Because of our background experiences, Philip and I simply move through life with different perceptions and expectations. Couples can't really avoid disconnects that are rooted in different cultural or socioeconomic backgrounds. We also can't avoid disconnects rooted in our different personalities or temperaments, such as being introverted or shy.

Arguing over these things is our way of overcoming the differences and connecting again despite them. I use the term *arguing* loosely here to refer to positive, productive discussions over things we disagree about, and not destructive patterns of fighting (like Gottman's deadly horsemen). If we can keep in mind our original vision of our spouse, it will help us remember what is most important about them to us. If we can cherish that vision, it will help us remain engaged, emotionally available, and respectful, even when we hit a bump in the road.

Even if I momentarily lose sight of my original revelation of Philip, eventually it becomes clear again. That central thing about him that captured my heart — his kindness and honesty — still rules his core. In our more than two decades of marriage, he has never intentionally said a cruel thing to me. When I've been sick or vulnerable, he's been protective and comforting. He makes me feel like I'm the only woman in the world for him. I know I can trust him with my heart and my life, and those of our children.

You may know more about your spouse today than you did the day you married him, but don't forget what may be the most important things about him — the things you *did* know on that day. When we choose to remember why we loved our spouse in the beginning, we can love them better today in order to protect the future we promised to each other.

Practice Radical Forgiveness

In a grace-filled marriage, we choose day by day to love our spouse like Christ loves him or her, like Christ loves the Church. How does Christ love the Church? Selflessly. Totally. Completely. If you practice this principle in your marriage, you will be blessed in countless ways. As Pope John Paul II explained to us:[11]

> [Spouses] are called to grow continually in their communion through day-to-day fidelity to their marriage promise of total mutual self-giving. … The gift of the Spirit is a commandment of life for Christian spouses and at the same time a stimulating impulse so that every day they may progress towards an ever richer union with each other on all levels — of the body, of the character, of the heart, of the intelligence and will, of the soul — revealing in this way to the Church and to the world the new communion of love, given by the grace of Christ.[11]

The mutual, generous kind of love that we're talking about here is the "we-love" (*philia*) which I introduced in chapter 1. In mutuality, both spouses commit to the wellbeing and flourishing of the other. We're both willing to give and receive love (rather than one person doing all the giving while others do all the receiving). We quietly look for ways to be Christ to one another.

Just as we don't want to wait until our children's attachment cups are running dry before we start filling them, we don't have to wait until our spouse expresses a need to meet it. We can anticipate what our spouse needs emotionally, physically, and practically, and be his answer. In surrendering ourselves for the good of the other, we paradoxically find our true selves.[12] The more I focus on helping Philip become the man God wants him to be, and less on my own plans and preoccupations, the more I become the woman God wants me to be. My own plans for myself can't compare to God's plans for me.

All of humanity needs to love and be loved like this. We all thirst for it — it was written on our hearts from the beginning, even before the Fall.[13] That's the kind of love God envisions for us as a married couple. Again, this doesn't mean we're a doormat. Sometimes loving Philip like Christ loves him means I will speak up and gently point out something he needs to hear. I'm as responsible for what I don't say out of cowardice as for what I do say in rashness.

When we build our marriage on Christ's example, even those inevitable disagreements seem to blow over quickly. When our spouse hurts us, it would be very human of us to offer tit for tat—to withdraw our generosity and love because it doesn't seem deserved. But we aren't stuck in our humanness. We have the graces of marriage to help us love supernaturally. We can love because Christ loves, and forgive because Christ forgives. When we're frustrated or angry with our spouse, we can recall that Christ loves *us* without counting the cost, without comparing his sacrifice to ours; he loves us *even though we don't deserve it.* None of us deserves it. Yet, he offers it to us generously and unconditionally. We offer our spouse this kind of love not because he deserves it, but because Christ loves him like this. So we pray for and practice patience, forbearance, and forgiveness.

While these tips are simple and powerful, they're not easy to practice. God understands this, and he gives us ample opportunities to learn and grow through the years. Discovering the joy in Catholic marriage is ultimately about our own choices. Each day, we choose in small ways to create a marriage that is a tabernacle of divine light, a fortress against darkness. When we love like Christ loves, when we forgive like he forgives, together we become a sign of the New Covenant. Because of the graces of marriage, we can be greater together than we ever could be apart.

The Joyful Catholic Home

The glory of God is a human person fully alive.
SAINT IRENAEUS

Ultimately, the path of family discipleship is a path of authentic joy, for kids and parents alike. We find joy together in many places and in many kinds of experiences. We discover it in the natural world, a place some of us forgot about until our kids dragged us over to look at a little burrow in the dirt beneath the backyard tree or a spider's web stretched across a window. It often washes over us during the last minutes before our little ones drift off to sleep when we can't help staring at them. As they grow up, we experience joy in watching them wrestle with and overcome new challenges in their development. We experience joy in these moments because we are encountering not just the loveliness of nature or these little people we love; we are encountering Christ-among-us.

For parents, joy comes in knowing we are right where we need to be, fulfilling the mission God has called us to do. It comes from our cooperation with God as he continues to create the world, including our children who are still coming to be themselves. What an incredible privilege. Even in the face of setbacks or suffering, we can possess a tranquility that is inexplicable because it is a divine gift. Joy is despair defeated. (The devil hates it when that happens.)

If you attend to the seven building blocks, you will begin to live more joyfully because you will be busy fulfilling your family's mission: building a community of life and love. You may not be positively giddy every day, but Christian joyfulness endures even when emotional happiness wanes. With this joy, we trust in a God who sustains us, we have hope in his promises, and we live with confidence that we are going to be okay.

I think this deeper joy is a clue to why the seven building blocks are so important. They are reminders of the truth about what really nourishes within our children a deep sense of safety about the world and a readiness for authentic friendship with others, including God. They remind us of what our children need in order to be fully alive, so they can recognize and cross the bridge of discipleship. Everywhere we turn, somebody is telling us how we should be spending our time or money. In a world that wants to sell us a lie about what our kids need and deserve, sometimes we just need a simple reminder. Our kids don't need or deserve the latest iPhone, expensive shoes, or Kylie Jenner lip gloss. Those are distractions from the truth, mere counterfeits of real love. Our children need and deserve deep connection to us, opportunities for play, lessons in virtue, wonder toward real beauty, and roots in their Catholic faith. Our kids need and deserve a chance to grow up drenched in authentic love so that they can recognize it out in the world — and can quickly spot its counterfeits.

Perfect Disciples Not Needed

Parenting is a powerful spiritual practice: It calls on us to exercise patience, mercy, and love; it invites us to mirth, wonder, and transformation; it requires us to surrender, forgive, and sometimes even suffer. We live out our practice in real moments with these little people who depend on us for The Answers. In this practice, sometimes we'll fail to surrender, to follow God's lead, or to give our children what they need even when we have it to give. Just remember that Christ's disciples were all sinners. They ran away and hid from their duties. They failed to recognize Christ when he was standing right in front of them after the Resurrection. And still Christ called them to build the Church. In our brokenness, we will doubt, hide, and fail as disciple-parents. And still Christ is calling us to build our little seminaries and raise holy disciples. He comforts us as he comforted Paul, "My grace is sufficient for you, for my power is made perfect in weakness" (2 Cor 12:9).

Your kids won't be perfect on this path of discipleship either. In fact, at some point in your Catholic parenting journey, your kids will say or do something that makes your brain hurt. Did you know that in religious communities, leaders have to navigate different personality types and conflicting needs and desires? You're the head of a spiritual community: your family. You are forming your little novitiates in virtue, mentoring them in recognizing and attending to the needs and feelings of others in your home, and guiding them in identifying God's mission for them. Tensions and frustration will be part of that process. Some days you will have no idea what you're doing. That's okay. Just nourish those attachment roots; be the answer to your children's deepest yearnings for connection. Prioritize your family relationships and you will make it through. Keep showing up, and in the long run, you will see fruit. You've got this.

Recognize Your Strengths and Weaknesses

As our time together ends, I invite you to reflect on the seven building blocks, and how you might begin living them out with your children. It's too overwhelming to think about everything you've read at once. Just start somewhere. Identify and celebrate your strengths: Which building blocks are strong in your parenting? Where are they working well in your family? Every parent possesses natural gifts or inherent personal traits that they bring to their relationship with their children and spouse. Perhaps by nature you are calm yet firm with your children, or personally committed to the health of your marriage. Thank God for these graces.

We also possess weaknesses or blind spots that make it harder for us to give our families what they need. What are your tendencies or habits that cause strife or disconnection in your home? Do you have any childhood wounds that are preventing you from loving fully and freely? Do you struggle with overcommitment? Does your family have any habits that need to be addressed? Do your children respect your boundaries and rules? Many of us take a wrong turn because we settle for what is "normal" in our culture, until we realize our family is suffering for it. Don't settle for normal anymore. What's normal out in the world is terribly unhealthy. Build up your joyful Catholic home even if your neighbors think you're weird!

Pick one building block to focus on this month. Do you need to think about bringing some balance into your home? Do your kids have too many commitments and not enough time for free play? Do you need some help with discipline? Just start somewhere, and invite God into your home as you begin to build a stronger domestic church. Then, next month, take an inventory and focus on a new building block.

You're never alone. Mary, mother of Jesus, experienced first-hand what it's like raising a family. She knows intimately every parent's hopes, delights, and fears at every stage of life. Jesus had to learn to talk and walk, to respect his parents, to put away his toys. He had to study, learn his manners, and navigate through hard talks with his friends and parents. My parish priest once pointed out that Jesus must have had acne when he was a teenager. Imagine that! Mary understands you. Entrust your family to her.

As you go, I leave you with this prayer for protection for

your family:

Holy Mary, Virgin Mother of God, you were conceived without sin. I choose you this day as the model for my household, and the intercessor for my family. Through your Immaculate Conception, preserve us from every disaster, from violence, and from misfortune. O Holy Virgin, bless and protect us all, strengthen us in trial, and save us from all evil. Amen.

Notes

INTRODUCTION

1. "Through the grace of the sacrament of marriage, parents receive the responsibility and privilege of *evangelizing their children*" (*Catechism of the Catholic Church* 2225).
2. "What is your religious preference?", General Social Survey (GSS), quoted in "Religion Among the Millennials," Pew Research Center, last modified February 17, 2010, http://www.pewforum .org/2010/02/17/religion-among-the-millennials/.
3. Charles J. Chaput, *Strangers in a Strange Land: Living the Catholic Faith in a Post-Christian World* (New York: Henry Holt, 2017).
4. Marcellino D'Ambrosio, *When the Church Was Young: Voices of the Early Fathers* (Cincinnati: Servant Books, 2014), 208.
5. This is the thesis of Gordon Neufeld and Gabor Maté in *Hold On to Your Kids: Why Parents Need to Matter More Than Peers* (New York: Ballantine Books, 2006).
6. United States Conference of Catholic Bishops, *Compendium of the Social Doctrine of the Church* (Washington, D.C.: Libreria Editrice Vaticana, 2004), par. 193.
7. Catholics are called to prioritize the needs of the weak, but weaker persons should be empowered to contribute to the "good of all" as they are able. See John Paul II's encyclical *Sollicitudo Rei Socialis* (The Concern of the Church for the Social Order), par. 39.

CHAPTER ONE

1. Edward Collins Vacek, SJ, explains the meaning and features of mutuality in "Philia," in *Love, Human and Divine: The Heart of Christian Ethics* (Washington, D.C.: Georgetown University Press, 1994), 280–319.
2. James W. Fowler, "Infancy and Undifferentiated Faith," in *Stages*

of Faith: The Psychology of Human Development and the Quest for Meaning, rev. ed. (New York: HarperOne, 1981), 119–121.

3. Adapted from Douglas Davies, *Child Development, Third Edition: A Practitioner's Guide* (New York: The Guilford Press, 2011), 8–11.

4. Daniel J. Siegel and Mary Hartzell, *Parenting from the Inside Out: How a Deeper Self-Understanding Can Help You Raise Children Who Thrive* (New York: Penguin, 2004), 68.

5. Margot Sunderland, *The Science of Parenting: How Today's Brain Research Can Help You Raise Happy, Emotionally Balanced Children* (New York: D. K. Publishing, 2008), 22.

6. Davies, *Child Development*, 9.

7. Jude Cassidy, "The Nature of the Child's Ties," in *Handbook of Attachment: Theory, Research, and Clinical Applications*, eds. J. Cassidy and P. R. Shaver (New York: Guilford Press, 2010), 3–22.

8. Gordon Neufeld, "The Attachment Factor" (recorded lecture, Neufeld Institute, *Intensive 1: Making Sense of Kids*, Session 10), accessed March 17, 2019.

9. Gordon Neufeld, "How Attachment Empowers" (recorded lecture, Neufeld Institute *Intensive 1*, Session 12), accessed March 4, 2019.

10. Davies, *Child Development*, 12–18.

11. "No expression of social life — from the family to intermediate social groups, associations, enterprises of an economic nature, cities, regions, States, up to the community of peoples and nations — can escape the issue of its own common good, in that this is the constitutive element of its significance and the authentic reason for its very existence." See United States Conference of Catholic Bishops, *Compendium of the Social Doctrine of the Church* (Washington, D.C.: Libreria Editrice Vaticana, 2004), par. 165.

12. *Gaudium et Spes* (Pastoral Constitution on the Church in the Modern World), Vatican website, December 7, 1965, Vatican.va, par. 26.

13. Pope John XXIII, *Pacem in Terris* (Peace on Earth), encyclical letter, Vatican website, April 11, 1963, w2.vatican.va, par. 57.

14. If you'd like to explore the benefits of the well-known tools of baby bonding, I highly recommend Greg and Lisa Popcak, *Then Comes Baby: The Catholic Guide to Surviving and Thriving in the First Three Years of Parenthood* (Notre Dame, IN: Ave Maria Press, 2014).

15. Bruce Perry and Maia Szalavitz, *Born for Love: Why Empathy Is Essential — and Endangered* (New York: William Morrow, 2010), 49.

16. This six-stage model is explored in depth in the Neufeld In-

stitute's *Intensive I: Making Sense of Kids* (neufieldinstitute.org), a
course I cite throughout this book. The model is explored, too, in
Gordon Neufeld's shorter course *The Attachment Puzzle*. See also his
book, *Hold On to Your Kids*, 20–25.
17. Gordon Neufeld, "How Children Are Meant to Attach" (recorded
lecture, Neufeld Institute *Intensive 1*, Session 11), accessed March 1,
2019.
18. Neufeld and Maté, *Hold On to Your Kids*, 24.
19. "No adequate assessment of the nature of the human person or
the requirements for human fulfillment and psycho-social well-being can be made without respect for man's spiritual dimension and
capacity for self-transcendence" (Pope John Paul II, "Address of His
Holiness John Paul II to the Members of the American Psychiatric
Association and the World Psychiatric Association," speech, Vatican
website, January 4, 1993, w2.vatican.va, par. 2).
20. "Only by transcending themselves and living a life of self-giving
and openness to truth and love can individuals reach fulfillment and
contribute to building an authentic human community" (John Paul II,
"Address to the Members of the APA and WPA," January 4, 1993).
21. Pehr Granqvist, "Attachment and Religiosity in Adolescence:
Cross-Sectional and Longitudinal Evaluations," *Personality and
Social Psychology Bulletin* 28, no. 2 (February 2002): 260–270,
doi:10.1177/0146167202282011.
22. See, for example, Angie McDonald et al., "Attachment to God and
Parents: Testing the Correspondence vs. Compensation Hypothe-
ses," *Journal of Psychology and Christianity* 24, no. 1 (2005): 21–28.
Students who grew up in "emotionally cold" homes were more likely
to be avoidant in their relationship with God; students who grew up
in rigid, authoritarian style homes were not only avoidant with God,
but they were also anxious about approaching God. I recognize the
limitations of this study. The participants were all Christian college
students, mostly Church of Christ members, so the sample was
fairly narrow. Still, it is fascinating and important.
23. William A. Barry, SJ, *Finding God in All Things: A Companion to
the Spiritual Exercises of St. Ignatius* (Notre Dame, IN: Ave Maria
Press, 1991), 22.
24. Sherry A. Weddell, *Forming Intentional Disciples: The Path to
Knowing and Following Jesus* (Huntington, IN: Our Sunday Visitor,
2012), 129.
25. "The adult's mind with respect to attachment is the most robust
predictor of a child's attachment" (Siegel and Hartzell, *Parenting*

from the Inside Out, 120–122).

26. Adapted from Siegel and Hartzell, "How We Make Sense of Our Lives: Adult Attachment," in *Parenting from the Inside Out*.

27. See Siegel and Hartzell, "How We Keep It Together and How We Fall Apart: The High Road and the Low Road," in *Parenting from the Inside Out*.

28. Gordon Neufeld, "The Tempering Effect" (recorded lecture, Neufeld Institute *Intensive 1*, Session 7), accessed February 16, 2019.

29. I first heard the notion of emotional temperature on Greg and Lisa Popcak's radio program, *More2Life*.

30. Siegel and Hartzell, *Parenting from the Inside Out*, 156–159.

CHAPTER TWO

1. Wilfrid Stinissen, OCD, *Eternity in the Midst of Time*, trans. Clare Marie, OCD (San Francisco: Ignatius Press, 2018), 85.

2. For example, see Bernadette Noll, *Slow Family Living: 75 Simple Ways to Slow Down, Connect, and Create More Joy* (New York: Penguin, 2013); and Kym John Payne, *Simplicity Parenting: Using the Extraordinary Power of Less to Raise Calmer, Happier, and More Secure Kids* (New York: Ballantine Books, 2009).

3. Gregory and Lisa Popcak, *Parenting with Grace: The Catholic Parents' Guide to Raising Almost Perfect Kids*, 2nd ed. (Huntington, IN: Our Sunday Visitor, 2010), 227.

4. Tuned-in mom Rachel Macy Stafford writes about unplugging from technology in order to connect better to her family in *Hands Free Mama: A Guide to Putting Down the Phone, Burning the To-Do List, and Letting Go of Perfection to Grasp What Really Matters!* (Grand Rapids, MI: Zondervan, 2013). See also her blog *Hands Free Mama* (www.handsfreemama.com).

5. On love of self as the basis for love of others, see James F. Keenan, SJ, *Moral Wisdom: Lessons and Texts from the Catholic Tradition*, 2nd ed. (New York: Rowman and Littlefield, 2010), 20–26.

6. "Sometimes we lose our enthusiasm for mission because we forget that the Gospel responds to our deepest needs, since we were created for what the Gospel offers us: friendship with Jesus and love of our brothers and sisters. ... It is impossible to persevere in a fervent evangelization unless we are convinced from personal experience that it is not the same thing to have known Jesus as not to have known him, not the same thing to walk with him as to walk blindly, not the same thing to hear his word as not to know it, and not the same thing to contemplate

him, to worship him, to find our peace in him, as not to. … A person who is not convinced, enthusiastic, certain and in love, will convince nobody" (Pope Francis, *Evangelii Gaudium* [The Joy of the Gospel], apostolic exhortation, Vatican website, November 24, 2013, w2.vatican .va, par. 265–266).

7. Genevieve Kineke, *The Authentic Catholic Woman* (Cincinnati: Servant Books, 2006), 127.

8. Stuart Brown, MD, *Play: How It Shapes the Brain, Opens the Imagination, and Invigorates the Soul* (New York: Avery, 2009), 71, 73.

9. Pope John Paul II, "The Angelus Reflections, 1995," in *The Genius of Women* (Washington, D.C.: United States Conference of Catholic Bishops, 1997), 27.

10. Gwen Dewar, PhD, "How Daycare Centers Change the Stress Response System (and What We Can Do About It)," Parenting Science, last modified July 9, 2009, https://www.parentingscience.com /daycare-centers.html.

CHAPTER THREE

1. Brown, *Play*, 5.

2. Kenneth R. Ginsburg, MD, MSEd, "The Importance of Play in Promoting Healthy Child Development and Maintaining Strong Parent-Child Bonds," *Pediatrics* 119, no. 1 (January 2007): 182.

3. Kim John Payne argues against allowing children younger than ten to play organized sports, especially to the exclusion of time for unstructured play, because that involvement "can cut crudely across their progression through a variety of play stages that are vitally important to development" (see Payne, *Simplicity Parenting*, 155–158).

4. My understanding of play and child development is drawn from Davies, *Child Development*.

5. A. N. Wilson, *C. S. Lewis: A Biography* (New York: Fawcett Columbine, 1990), 12.

6. Lawrence J. Cohen, PhD, *Playful Parenting: An Exciting New Approach to Raising Children That Will Help You Nurture Close Connections, Solve Behavior Problems, and Encourage Confidence* (New York: Ballantine Books, 2001), 4.

7. So much so that Dutch medievalist Johan Huizinga titles his classic examination of play in different societies *Homo Ludens*, Man the Player. He argues that play is the primary (though not only) element of those cultures that survive and thrive.

8. Cohen, *Playful Parenting*, 56.

9. Thomas Aquinas, *Summa Theologica*, IIa-IIae, q. 168, art. 2.

10. If you are looking for guidance on the appropriateness of contemporary films for your family movie nights, I suggest Decent Films – SDG Reviews (www.decentfilms.com), written by Catholic film critic Steven Greydanus. He evaluates films for their artistic and moral value.

11. My son Dominic was such a keen card player when he was a little boy that I had to expand my repertoire of card games! I found help in Alfred Sheinwold's *101 Best Family Card Games* (New York: Sterling, 1992).

12. Sunderland, *The Science of Parenting*, 147.

13. Family Pastimes sells several good cooperative games. Our favorites are *Snow Storm* and *Secret Door*. See also Josette Luvmour's *Everyone Wins!: Cooperative Games and Activities*, new ed. (Gabriola Island, BC, Canada: New Society Publishers, 2007).

14. Gordon Neufeld discusses futility in "The Adaptive Process" (recorded lecture, Neufeld Institute, *Intensive 1: Making Sense of Kids*, Session 4). Children need to face futility in order to become resilient and creative in the face of obstacles.

15. Payne, *Simplicity Parenting*, 98.

16. For insights into play theology, I benefited greatly from Jürgen Moltmann's incomparable *Theology of Play*, trans. Reinhard Ulrich (New York: Harper & Row, 1972). My understanding is also informed by Brian Edgar, *The God Who Plays* (Eugene, OR: Cascade Books, 2017); David L. Miller, *Gods & Games: Toward a Theology of Play* (New York: Harper Colophon, 1973); and Robert K. Johnston, *The Christian at Play* (Grand Rapids, MI: W.B. Eerdmans, 1983).

17. Moltmann, *Theology of Play*, 3.

18. C. S. Lewis, *Surprised by Joy: The Shape of My Early Life* (Orlando, FL: Harcourt, 1955), 173.

19. Lewis, *Surprised by Joy*, 13–14.

20. "Play having opened him up to the possibility of relating directly to Joy itself, Lewis later found Joy to be fully actualized in his personal experience with Jesus Christ" (Johnston, *The Christian at Play*, 77).

CHAPTER FOUR

1. Deborah MacNamara, *Rest, Play, Grow: Making Sense of Preschoolers (Or Anyone Who Acts Like One)* (Vancouver, Canada: Aona Books, 2016), 224.

2. "[O]ur entire theological tradition is expressed in terms of mercy — that is, the willingness to enter into the chaos of others so as to answer them in their need" (Keenan, *Moral Wisdom*, 121).

3. Davies, *Child Development*, 292.

4. For a sustained explication of Thomas Aquinas's view of the emotions, see Nicholas E. Lombardo, OP, *The Logic of Desire: Aquinas on Emotion* (Washington, D.C.: The Catholic University of America Press, 2010).

5. "In themselves passions are neither good nor evil. They are morally qualified only to the extent that they effectively engage reason and will" (CCC 1767).

6. For example, the German philosopher Immanuel Kant believed human feelings are pathological and have no role in living a moral life. Even Saint Bonaventure believed we have to force our emotions into submission. For these thinkers, emotions have to be subdued by the rational mind like a kind of dictator ruling over a slave.

7. "It has always been held that only the unrelenting training of the will could enable us to be virtuous. However, virtue consists of habitual perfecting and ordering of the principles, the building blocks, of a human act. Since these principles are both will and emotions, and not the will alone, it follows that the cultivation of the emotions is as important as the thorough education of reason and the strengthening of the will in the development of the virtues." See Conrad W. Baars, *Feeling & Healing Your Emotions: A Christian Psychiatrist Shows You How to Grow to Wholeness* (Gainesville, FL: Bridge Logos, 2003), 76.

8. Another interesting point: Whether our anger is bad also depends on the object of our anger. If I'm angry because my friend got a new car and I didn't, then this is bad; but if I'm angry because an innocent woman is being beaten in front of me, then this is righteous anger.

9. Tim Clinton and Gary Sibcy, *Attachments: Why You Love, Feel, and Act the Way You Do* (Brentwood, TN: Integrity Publishers, 2002), 181.

10. Sarah Ockwell-Smith, *Gentle Discipline: Using Emotional Connection — Not Punishment — to Raise Confident, Capable Kids* (New York: Penguin Random House, 2017), 1.

11. See Neufeld and Gabor Maté's groundbreaking book *Hold On to Your Kids: Why Parents Need to Matter More Than Peers* (New York: Ballantine Books, 2006). He also offers online seminars for counselors, teachers, and parents at the Neufeld Institute (neufeldinstitute.

org).

12. Neufeld and Maté, *Hold On to Your Kids*, 9.

13. Gordon Neufeld, "Taming an Alpha Complex" (recorded lecture, Neufeld Institute, *Alpha Children*, Session 4).

14. Neufeld and Maté, *Hold On to Your Kids*, 194–195.

15. Ibid., 183–184.

16. Gordon Neufeld, "Peer Orientation: Why Adults Must Matter More Than Peers" (speech, KMT Child Development Learning and Community Conference, Toronto, April 13, 2012).

17. Gordon Neufeld, "The Integrative Process" (recorded lecture, Neufeld Institute, *Intensive 1: Making Sense of Kids*, Session 6), accessed February 12, 2019.

18. See, for example, Nicholas Kardaras, *Glow Kids: How Screen Addiction Is Hijacking Our Kids — and How to Break the Trance* (New York: St. Martin's Press, 2016).

19. Here I'm bringing together the psychosocial developmental model of Erik Erikson and insights from the cognitive sciences about brain development in children. Unless otherwise noted, I'm relying on Davies, *Child Development*; and Christopher Peterson and Martin E.P. Seligman, *Character Strengths and Virtues: A Handbook and Classification* (New York: Oxford University Press, 2004).

20. Sunderland, *The Science of Parenting*, 20.

21. Ockwell-Smith, *Gentle Discipline*, 36.

22. This term was coined in the 1960s by the renowned Harvard developmentalist Sheldon White.

23. Here I'm bringing together and adapting Gordon Neufeld's six-phase attachment model and the psychological hungers originally identified by Eric Berne, founder of transactional analysis.

24. United States Conference of Catholic Bishops, *Compendium of the Social Doctrine of the Church* (Washington, D.C.: Libreria Editrice Vaticana, 2004), par. 189–191.

25. "Human virtues acquired by education, by deliberate acts and by a perseverance ever-renewed in repeated efforts are purified and elevated by divine grace. With God's help, they forge character and give facility in the practice of the good. The virtuous man is happy to practice them" (CCC 1810).

26. Thomas Dubay, SM, *The Evidential Power of Beauty: Science and Theology Meet* (San Francisco: Ignatius Press, 1999), 244.

27. If you'd like to read more about virtue education, start with Peter Kreeft, *Back to Virtue: Traditional Moral Wisdom for Modern Moral Confusion* (San Francisco: Ignatius Press, 1992); and Romano Guar-

dini, *Learning the Virtues: That Lead You to God* (Manchester, NH: Sophia Institute Press, 1967). To read with your children: William Bennett's books *The Book of Virtues* (New York: Simon & Schuster, 1993) and *The Children's Book of Virtues* (New York: Simon & Schuster, 1995).

28. "Virtue consists of the habitual perfecting and ordering of the principles, the building blocks, of a human act. Since these principles are both will and emotions, and not the will alone, it follows that the cultivation of the emotions is as important as a thorough education of reason and the strengthening of the will in the development of the virtues" (Baars, *Feeling & Healing Your Emotions*, 76).

29. For more help on follow-through and physical redirection, see especially Dr. Gregory and Lisa Popcak, *Parenting with Grace*, 134–136; and Jane Nelsen, *Positive Discipline for Preschoolers: For Their Early Years — Raising Children Who Are Responsible, Respectful, and Resourceful* (New York: Three Rivers Press, 2007), 175–181.

30. Cohen, *Playful Parenting*.

31. Not all tears are healthy, of course. Tears that come from a feeling of abandonment or terror are signs of mistreatment, not maturity.

32. Gordon Neufeld, "The Adaptive Process" (recorded lecture, Neufeld Institute, *Intensive 1*, Session 5), accessed February 10, 2019.

33. When kids are mature enough to understand the lesson, clarify that there is a difference between feeling an emotion and brooding over perceived wrongs. Holding on to anger, jealousy, or irritation and ruminating on it until it impacts your behavior is very unhealthy and possibly sinful. The Church teaches us that it's not a sin to feel anger, but if you nurse your hatred until you become bitter, then it's wrong. When we're overcome with anger so that it possesses our thoughts, when we find ourselves planning or obsessing about harming another person either physically or emotionally, or when we permit anger to fester into an irritable or violent disposition, then we've crossed the line. See CCC 2302.

CHAPTER FIVE

1. Perry and Szalavitz, *Born for Love*.

2. Perry and Szalavitz, *Born for Love*, 288.

3. Freda Mary Oben, *The Life and Thought of St. Edith Stein* (New York: Alba House, 2001), 104–105; Frances Horner, "Edith Stein on Empathy and Suffering," formerly available at www.carmelstream .com.

4. Horner, "Edith Stein on Empathy and Suffering."

5. "Through perceiving what is actualized in other persons each person learns what they are or are not in relation to others and comes to know their own unrealized potential." See Eric McClellan, "Edith Stein: Her Empathic Theology of the Human Person," *Pacifica: Australasian Theological Studies* 30, no. 1 (October 2017): 20–41, doi:10.1177%2F1030570X17725919.

6. This is my own extension of Stein's insight. Stein does not acknowledge any role of psychology or developmental science in her philosophy of empathy.

7. University of Michigan, "Empathy: College Students Don't Have As Much As They Used To, Study Finds," Science Daily, last modified May 19, 2010, www.sciencedaily.com /releases/2010/05/100528081434.htm. The original study was based on self-reporting (the Interpersonal Reactivity Index). Self-reporting can sometimes produce misleading outcomes, because participants may report what they believe is socially acceptable rather than how they actually behave. So, for example, some self-reports on dieting can be unreliable. But in this Michigan study, the participants were self-reporting on their feelings of concern for others; it appears to be a relatively strong measure. If anything, in such a study, the most likely inaccuracy would be participants exaggerating their empathic responses. In addition, the same index was used for incoming freshmen for thirty years.

8. Ibid.

9. Some colleges, such as Franciscan University of Steubenville, have become so concerned with the impact of technology on the building of community that the administration actively discourages students from taking out their phones while they are walking around campus. They encourage students to look up and acknowledge one another in passing. This is basic neighborliness. When I was at Franciscan recently for an event, I was impressed when I realized I hadn't seen a single student talking on or looking at their device while walking through the campus! Refreshing!

10. See Neufeld and Maté, *Hold On to Your Kids.*

11. MacNamara, *Rest, Play, Grow,* 136.

12. Gordon Neufeld, "How to Keep Children Safe in a Wounding World" (recorded address, Neufeld Institute *Intensive 1: Making Sense of Kids,* Session 9), accessed February 25, 2019.

13. Weddell, *Forming Intentional Disciples,* 136.

14. Robert Karen, *Becoming Attached: First Relationships and How*

They Shape Our Capacity to Love, repr. ed. (New York: Oxford University Press, 1998), 185, 195, 199. (Note that the most empathic children have secure attachments to both parents.) Science journalist Gwen Dewar, PhD, suggests that, because securely attached children grow up in "oxytocin friendly" homes, and because oxytocin has been linked to our ability to read the emotions of others just by looking at their eyes, it's possible that all those oxytocin-promoting parenting practices like cuddling and hugging help our kids' brains get primed for reading the feelings of others. See her article "The Case for Teaching Empathy: Why Empathy Doesn't 'Just Happen,'" Parenting Science, last modified 2013, https://www.parentingscience.com/teaching-empathy.html, citing numerous scientific studies.

15. Sunderland, *The Science of Parenting*, 230.
16. Gordon Neufeld, "The Emergent Process" (recorded lecture, Neufeld Institute, *Intensive 1*, Session 3), accessed February 7, 2019.
17. MacNamara, *Rest, Play, Grow,* 136.
18. Quoted in Karen, *Becoming Attached*, 195.
19. John Gottman, *Raising an Emotionally Intelligent Child: The Heart of Parenting* (New York: Simon & Schuster, 1997), 50–68.
20. Gordon Neufeld, "Heart Matters: What to Do with a Child's Feelings" (recorded address, Neufeld Institute, *Intensive 1*, September 24, 2013), accessed February 2, 2019.
21. Gordon Neufeld, "The Tempering Effect" (recorded lecture, Neufeld Institute, *Intensive 1*, Session 7), accessed February 16, 2019.
22. Dr. Laura Markham, *Peaceful Parent, Happy Siblings: How to Stop the Fighting and Raise Friends for Life* (New York: Perigree, 2015), 80.
23. Gottman, *Raising an Emotionally Intelligent Child*, 127.

CHAPTER SIX

1. The most important book that led to my reversion was Aidan Nichols, OP, *The Holy Eucharist: From the New Testament to Pope John Paul II* (Eugene, OR: Wipf & Stock, 2011), which traces the history of Eucharistic theology from the first through the twentieth centuries.
2. "Approximately one-third of the survey respondents who say they were raised Catholic no longer describe themselves as Catholic. This means that roughly 10 percent of all Americans are former Catholics." See "The Impact of Religious Switching and Secularization on the Estimated Size of the U.S. Adult Catholic Population," Center for

Applied Research in the Apostolate, last modified 2008, http://cara
.georgetown.edu/CARAServices/FRStats/Winter2008.pdf.
3. "What is Your Religious Preference?," General Social Survey
(GSS), quoted in "Religion Among the Millennials," Pew Research
Center, last modified February 17, 2010, http://www.pewforum
.org/2010/02/17/religion-among-the-millennials/.
4. Cardinal Sean P. O'Malley, quoted in "Church Must Foster Encounter with Culture, Cardinals Say," Catholic News Agency, last
modified November 21, 2013, http://www.catholicnewsagency.com
/news/church-must-foster-encounter-with-culture-cardinals-say.
5. Robert Louis Wilken, "The Church as Culture," *First Things* (April
2004), https://www.firstthings.com/article/2004/04/the-church-as
-culture.
6. For example, see Bishop Barron, "Catholicism and Beauty," You-
Tube video, 1:01:42, from a talk at the 2018 Los Angeles Religious
Education Congress, posted by Bishop Robert Barron, March 26,
2018, https://www.youtube.com/watch?v=iUBNTNiqn60.
7. Hans Urs van Balthasar is best known for his "trilogy," 17 volumes
on the transcendentals of being, divided into three parts: part 1,
The Glory of the Lord, on beauty/aesthetics; part 2, *Theo-Drama*, on
goodness/morality; part 3, *Theo-Logic*, on truth.
8. Because we homeschool, when my children are old enough to
study art history, I have a Catholic art history curriculum, which
gives me the tools I need to teach them systematically. See Bethany
Pederson, *Ever Ancient, Ever New: Art History, Appreciation, Theory,
and Practice*, available from Catholic Heritage Curricula
(www.chcweb.com).
9. Dubay, *The Evidential Power of Beauty*, 56.
10. Wilken, "The Church as Culture."
11. Mary Reed Newland, *The Year and Our Children: Catholic Family
Celebrations for Every Season* (Manchester, NH: Sophia Institute
Press, 2007), xi.
12. *Christian Prayer: The Liturgy of the Hours* (New York: Catholic
Book Publishing, 1976).
13. *Shorter Christian Prayer: The Four-Week Psalter of the Liturgy of
the Hours Containing Morning Prayer and Evening Prayer* (Totowa,
NJ: Catholic Book Publishing, 1999).
14. iBreviary.com in the U.S.; universalis.com in the UK.
15. See Jared Dees, *Lectio Divina for Children and Teens: Activities
to Help Young People Encounter God's Word*, The Religion Teacher,
https://www.thereligionteacher.com/lectio-divina-children-teens/.

16. Adapted from James W. Fowler, *Stages of Faith: The Psychology of Human Development and the Quest for Meaning*, rev. ed. (New York: HarperOne, 1981).

17. The "habit of wondering" in children and how it enhances their religious development is described nicely by Sofia Cavalletti in *The Religious Potential of the Child: Experiencing Scripture and Liturgy With Young Children* (Chicago: Archdiocese of Chicago: Liturgy Training Publications, 1992); see especially chapter 8, "Education to Wonder."

18. Gregory K. Popcak and Lisa Popcak, *Discovering God Together: The Catholic Guide to Raising Faithful Kids* (Manchester, NH: Sophia Institute Press, 2015), 53.

19. You might also enjoy R. Scott Hurd, *When Faith Feels Fragile: Help for the Wary, Weak, and Wandering* (Boston: Pauline Books & Media, 2013).

20. "The mode of Christ's presence under the Eucharistic species is unique. It raises the Eucharist above all the sacraments as 'the perfection of the spiritual life and the end to which all the sacraments tend.' In the most blessed sacrament of the Eucharist 'the body and blood, together with the soul and divinity, of our Lord Jesus Christ and, therefore, *the whole Christ is truly, really, and substantially* contained'" (CCC 1374).

21. For example, Mark Hart's series *Altaration: The Mystery of the Mass Revealed* (available at https://ascensionpress.com/collections /altaration-the-mystery-of-the-mass-revealed) is specifically for teenagers, and it's very well-done and powerful. It's a little pricey, but I can't recommend it highly enough. Your parish faith formation office might have it to loan out. Father Mike Schmitz's YouTube videos (available on the channel "Ascension Presents," (https://www. youtube.com/watch?v=MsqVeLPvsvU&list=PLeXS0cAkuTPpJ6j3e-H59WudJhJ4q1tpwH) are also lighthearted and fun for teenagers.

22. My reflection on the Eucharistic life is inspired by Alexander Schmemann, *The Eucharist: Sacrament of the Kingdom* (Yonkers, NY: St. Vladimir's Seminary Press, 1988); and Henri J. M. Nouwen, *With Burning Hearts: A Meditation on the Eucharistic Life* (Maryknoll, NY: Orbis Books, 1996).

23. Nouwen, *With Burning Hearts*, 89.

24. Some of my favorites: Catholic All Year (catholicallyear.com) and Shower of Roses (showerofrosesblog.com).

CHAPTER SEVEN

1. John Paul II, *Familiaris Consortio*, apostolic exhortation, Vatican website, November 22, 1981, w2.vatican.va, par. 13, emphasis mine.

2. If you are facing serious marital problems such as emotional or physical abuse, addiction, or infidelity, please seek help through your parish or a marriage counselor.

3. Dr. Sue Johnson, *Created for Connection: The "Hold Me Tight" Guide for Christian Couples* (New York: Little, Brown: 2016), 27–30.

4. Archibald D. Hart and Sharon Hart May, *Safe Haven Marriage: Building a Relationship You Want to Come Home To* (Nashville, TN: Thomas Nelson, 2003), 6.

5. Two books that helped me on this journey: Gregory Popcak, *For Better Forever: A Catholic Guide to Lifelong Marriage*, rev. ed. (Huntington, IN: Our Sunday Visitor, 2015); and Hart and May, *Safe Haven Marriage*.

6. John Gottman, *The Seven Principles for Making Marriage Work: A Practical Guide from the Country's Foremost Relationship Expert*, rev. ed. (New York: Harmony Books, 2015), 31.

7. Gottman, *The Seven Principles for Making Marriage Work*, 32.

8. Hart and May, *Safe Haven Marriage*, 29.

9. Robert Browning, "Meeting at Night."

10. Charles Williams, *The Figure of Beatrice: A Study in Dante* (London: Faber & Faber, 1943), especially chapter 3, "The Death of Beatrice." Sister Margaret A. Farley expounds upon Williams's notion of the "original revelation" in *Personal Commitments: Beginning, Keeping, Changing*, rev. ed. (New York: Orbis Books, 2013), 62–66.

11. Pope John Paul II, *Familiaris Consortio*, par. 19.

12. "This likeness reveals that man, who is the only creature on earth which God willed for itself, cannot fully find himself except through a sincere gift of himself" (*Gaudium et Spes*, par. 24).

13. Pope John Paul II, "The Nuptial Meaning of the Body," general audience, Vatican website, January 9, 1980, w2.vatican.va.

About the Author

KIM CAMERON-SMITH is the founder of the Intentional Catholic Parenting online ministry and the host of the Gentle Catholic Parenting Podcast, where she explores the intersection between Catholicism and the science of parenting. Her understanding of what it means to be an intentional Catholic parent continually grows and evolves as she learns more about her children, herself, and how God has created us to find him in all things, especially relationships. Kim is a licensed attorney and a member of the California State Bar. She received a B.A. in English from Wellesley College, an M.Phil. in Medieval Literature from Oxford University, a Master of Theological Studies from Harvard University, and a J.D. from U.C. Berkeley. She lives in Northern California with her husband, Philip, and their four children. You can find her at kimcameronsmith.com.